[   ]

[boxhead]

Darren O'Donnell

Coach House Books
Toronto

first edition

For production enquiries or just to chat, please contact Darren at darren@mammalian.ca.

  Canada Council for the Arts   Conseil des Arts du Canada   ONTARIO ARTS COUNCIL CONSEIL DES ARTS DE L'ONTARIO   Canada

Published with the generous assistance of the Canada Council for the Arts and the Ontario Arts Council. Coach House Books also acknowledges the support of the Government of Canada through the Book Publishing Industry Development Program.

LIBRARY AND ARCHIVES CANADA CATALOGUING IN PUBLICATION

O'Donnell, Darren, 1965-
    Boxhead / Darren O'Donnell. -- 1st ed.

A play.
ISBN 978-1-55245-210-3

    I. Title.

PS8579.D64B69 2008   c812'.6   C2008-906014-8

I'm most proud of the fact that *[boxhead]* wasn't my idea; the theatrical challenge of a show entirely about a guy with a box on his head was something that came from director Chris Abraham and actor Paul Fauteux. As far as Chris remembers it, they were working on Peter Handke's *Kaspar*, and dealing with language and reason as a kind of prison, game or box for the character. They approached me to work with them on a new project because Chris was curious to see how I would respond to the very actorly Paul. I'm always cranky about representational theatre, so trying to throw stuff that would irritate Paul became a primary motivation for me. I'm proud of all of this because it was the first large-scale collaboration on my part, the first time I had taken someone's constraints, run with them and come up with something better than any of us could have generated alone.

But back to irritating Paul. At the time, he was my idea of the worst sort of actor: National Theatre School trained, with a need to understand every line, a desire for every word to make sense; he insisted on comprehending what he was saying at every point, as if this were, somehow, the standard human condition. Which was a problem for me, since I had no clear idea of what the hell the show was about and was defiantly proud of that fact.

Chris was little help in this matter, searching as he always seems to be for a one-to-one relation between the things that happen in the show and a subconscious rationale that was completely clear, clean and transparent to consciousness. You know, what directors are supposed to do. I thought it was too Freudian an approach, excavating the text for the 'real' explanation behind the bizarre things that were happening. I wanted to create a show that would remain outside the grasp of rational thought, that questioned the boxheadedness of this acutely rational approach to life and hovered just outside of the audience's understanding. It seemed to me, however, that to attempt this while still completely understanding the show myself was impossible. If I could rationally comprehend the show, then, chances were, the audience could too. So the three of us scrapped a lot, while still having a respectful fun; in the end, this collaborative tension between us produced what has become my most successful play.

Collaboration is a tricky business. One of its exciting paradoxes is that one's success in a collaborative endeavour is often inversely proportional to the assertion of your own agenda – or, to put it the other way around, it's directly proportional to your ability to put your agenda on hold and incorporate others' desires and insights. But there are a lot of personal-issue pitfalls that can interfere with this seemingly easy task:

1 The narcissism of small differences, Freud's term for that tendency to dislike those who most remind you of yourself. The only way through this, it seems to me, is a sort of spiritual acceptance that things are the way they are: your current collaborators are the only collaborators you could possibility be working with since they are, in fact, staring at you from across the table.

2 Rejecting an idea because it's not yours. That's a famous one. The better the idea, the more comprehensive the rejection.

3 The inability to tell someone that his or her idea sucks. This is a basic skill that needs to be mastered, and really good collaborations develop techniques for this. In my previous company, Pow Pow Unbound, we used to have a little song about how stupid the person was.

4 The inability to propose an idea you know is bad. Bad ideas often contain the seeds of good ideas, so it's best to blurt them out and enjoy the ridicule.

5 Thin skin.

6 The tendency to enjoy compliments over criticism.

7 Fear of failure. An obvious one, but no less obvious should be the fact that an easy way to raise your success rate is to raise your failure rate. Fail often: take more risks and make more mistakes – eventually you're bound to succeed at something. It's a statistical fact.

As I've mentioned, the initial idea for *[boxhead]* came from Chris and Paul, but another key individual was actor/playwright Alex Poch-Goldin, who gave me a challenging bit of pre-emptive criticism when he poked at me about my anti-racism polemic, *White Mice*, asking which 'issue' I was going to tackle next. This was at the height of Issue Mania, when it was tough to find art that wasn't engaged with one prefabricated issue or another. *White Mice* certainly was an issue play, but one that I felt came honestly and had nothing to do with opportunism. Fuck you, Alex, I thought, and I resolved to make sure not only that the next show would not be an issue play, but that I would make an issue of it by writing the stupidest thing I could manage. Without Alex's collaborative participation, *[boxhead]* might have ended up being a show about, say, living with the disability of a box on your head. Luckily, Alex intervened, and we ended up with a show that climaxed with a fading god tricking a cloned geneticist into showing his penis to the audience so that the god can siphon off some of the audience's riveted attention in order to live longer.

Which brings me to that particular moment in the show. I believe it's fully rationalized and a logically necessary part of the story, but, in the interest of full disclosure, it began as simply a desire to demonstrate how weak we are when a naked penis is in the room – few people are able to drag their eyes off this slightly stinky tag of flesh. This, it seemed to me, was just another manifestation of humanity's (or a particular humanity's) boxheadedness. The magnetic-like attraction of a naked cock might have something to do with cultural phallocentrism or something else, but, whatever it is, it certainly is a sociocultural construction and a really funny one. I'm a bit of an exhibitionist, as any of my friends can tell you – not because it gives me any sexual charge, but because the whole prohibition against public nudity – our natural state – is so funny and puritanical that it requires constant ridicule.

Anywayyyyy. Collaboration. Theatre is often quite an atomized affair, with various elements of a play being designed in isolation and without the participation of others. This leads to some funny situations. We see fully designed costumes that the actors have to accept with little input, sets that are completed before actors take their first step, and whole conceptual themes that are imposed long before first rehearsal. This lack of faith in the collaborative process is driven by expediency, as time is at a premium and anything that can be nailed down and quantified is, and as soon as possible. A classic scenario is the moment following the first read-through, when the director turns to the stage manager and asks how long the show ran. Stopwatches often direct shows, with the core of the creative team unable to trust their feeling on the pace of the show. If it feels slow, it IS slow – a stopwatch will not be able to change that feeling, no matter what information it provides. It's common for the stopwatch to take over the role of the director and it can end up dictating adjustments to pace based entirely on some notion of the ideal time the show should occupy. It's faithlessness that drives this, a boxheaded disavowal of our intuitions and a dependence on a tired scientific rationalism that is capable of telling us very specific things – the show ran fifteen seconds faster than yesterday – but things that are empty of any real meaning. It also leads to other neuroticisms, like the fetish for arriving on time. Adopting the attitude that collaborators will arrive always at the correct time – whether they're late or not – has meant that the time spent waiting for them (when a traditional approach might be to get all freaked out about their lack of respect) provides time to get to know each other, shoot the shit and stumble upon ideas that might not have manifested had the offending collaborator arrived punctually.

With *[boxhead]*, an atypical collaborative relationship is necessary between the actors and the stage manager as they coordinate the complicated interplay of the different voices. Each actor plays two characters: the doctor and the doctor's narrator. Very often there is a complicated choreography of button-pushing on the vocal effects technology. Stephen Souter, the late, great stage manager, was the first person to tackle the task. He stuck a colour-coded circle beside each and every line in the script and on each button of the effects box and would carefully follow along, making hundreds of precisely timed switches. In that draft of the script, each actor played three characters, so at times there were six vocal settings. He, and subsequently Beth Kates, had to be completely on the ball, remaining as focused as the actors, the three of them working this tight choreography to create the illusion that there are multiple characters in constant conflict. This choreography is a very delicate thing that also happens to be travelling at an intense clip; as actor Adam Lazarus points out, 'There's somewhat of an unforgiving focus demanded – one missed word, a pause, a reorder, an extended breath, throws the show out of sync for ten minutes.'

The entire experience for the performer is something that materializes some of the themes of the show. I wanted to create something that went beyond merely representing a post-rational state and actually forced the performer into a state where they had to abandon their rational mind and fully accept the groove of the show. The split of consciousness required by acting can be an amazing thing to watch – an actor can sometimes appear to be fully engaged in a complicated discussion or choreography while in her head she might be assembling tomorrow's grocery list. But, inspired by the writings of E. J. Gold, who was, in turn, inspired by G. I. Gurdjieff, I wanted to create an experience for the actor that would be so overwhelming that it would be impossible to concentrate on anything else, so that the constant obsessive yammering in my head that provides the soundtrack to my life would stop and I could simply plug into the machine of the show and tune out of life. Gold and Gurdjieff both have techniques and exercises to overload the conscious mind, in order to let intuition run the human biological machine, as Gold calls it. Actors are often told not to overthink, to simply get in there and do. That's easy to say. [boxhead] was designed to make this happen by giving the actor as much to deal with as possible: complicated text, multiple characters and a detailed and complex physicality that is often at odds with what is being spoken, as the actor's voice has to portray one character while his body portrays another.

Paul Fauteux, the original boxhead: '[boxhead] is a very unique performance experience. It is not acting in the traditional sense. It is a concentration exercise. The exercise is created by the layers of disorientation which must be focused through while performing: the box on the head, through which we can see only dimly when it is tilted down and only the inside of the box when we are looking up; having to reach very precise locations onstage in the blackouts while we can barely see; the rhythmic, very imaginative, often non-linear language; the precise physicality; the fact that our voices are treated so we hear our own voices in the box and another voice going out to the audience simultaneously; the abrupt switches from one character to another – all these layers of focus create a trance-like zone of hyper-concentration which is extremely satisfying because it moves the actors' imaginations past the intellectual into the subconscious and throws them directly into the immediate.'

Adam Lazarus: 'The box is heavy, hot, humid; you hear voices, you can't see. It's like having a box on your head.'

The set was initially designed by Cand Cod – an anagram of the first initials of Darren O'Donnell, Chris Abraham and then-producer of the show Naomi Campbell. The great thing about working with a couple of people who have little experience in a given medium – in this case, set design – is that we didn't have very much attachment to our identities as set designers, yielding a relaxed productivity, where small suggestions, large concepts and final touches would just bubble to the surface as we hung out and got the show made. It was the same when Naomi and I worked on *White Mice* – just casual conversations between two people who have worked with sets all their lives but who don't know anything about designing them. This loose amateurism yielded a great design that was totally organic and relaxed. Small collaborations created simply to get things done can often make big differences. David Kinsman, the publicist at Theatre Passe Muraille, did a final and lasting tweak on the title when he encased it in square brackets. So great and so obvious, but no one but David saw it.

Chris brought on Romano De Nillo, the percussionist who created the sound score, which turned out to be a massively important element in the show. It was great to watch them work: Chris would describe feelings for accents, stings and scoring and Romano would toss stuff back. It's as close as I've ever seen to a couple of artists hanging out, like they were just a couple of guys jamming in some basement, but while in the pressure cooker of a brief rehearsal period. This relationship owed a lot to Romano's ridiculous relaxedness (he's an Italian Newfie) and Chris's brilliance at leading large groups of collaborators, tapping and making room for people's strengths. There weren't supposed to be any songs in the production – the first staging had maybe two. But this element worked so well that with each subsequent incarnation we've added a couple of numbers, always tweaking the satire so it remains current.

One of the collaborators I've always been keen to engage is the audience, looking for ways to rigorously include them in a way that isn't mortifying, embarrassing or dorky. The solution for [boxhead] was small but decisive: it would be the audience's responsibility to provide the key to the doctors' dilemma by pulling the rope that drops their compatibility results, revealing why they have been unable to conceive a baby. This moment is a second-rate rip-off of Brooks' and Verdecchia's *Noam Chomsky Lectures*, where they leave the responsibility for the show's final cue to the audience, who must call for a blackout, an onus we experience as analogous to the more general responsibility Daniel and Guillermo are laying on us throughout the show. Back in the day, that moment blew my mind: rigorous audience participation that perfectly expressed the themes of the show. In *[boxhead]*, the real-world stakes are decidedly lower, but for the four characters onstage, it's a crucial moment that has yielded either an incredibly nervous tension in the room or audience members leaping over one another to pull the rope. It's a small but important moment of audience collaboration; as I've argued elsewhere,[1] the active presence of the audience is pretty much the only positive factor that distinguishes theatre from film, video and television.

One of the problems at work in the way theatre artists usually think about collaboration is the conception of a theatre production as an organic totality. New York–based Mexican-born philosopher Manuel DeLanda points out that organic totalities are closed systems in which relations of interiority create a situation where component parts are constituted by the very relations they have to the whole: 'A part detached from such a whole ceases to be what it is, since being this particular part is one of the constitutive properties. A whole in which the component parts are self-subsistent and their relations as external to each other does not posses an organic unity.'[2] A theatre production is an organic totality, with the component parts not possessing any meaning if they're detached from the other parts. The actor cannot meaningfully speak those lines in any other context, the costume designs remain on the drawing board if they're not realized in the production, and a given sound montage is only valuable when it's in relation to the particular line and actions of a particular actor playing a particular part. There is a paradox of an atomized dependence in traditional theatre that forecloses fluid, flexible and autonomous collaboration.

---

1 *Social Acupuncture: A Guide to Suicide, Performance and Utopia* (Toronto: Coach House Books, 2006).

2 Manuel DeLanda, *A New Philosophy of Society: Assemblage Theory and Social Complexity* (London: Continuum International Publishing Group, 2006), 9.

These insights have been driven by my time spent working with various visual artists, particularly the Instant Coffee collective. When I worked with Jinhan Koh, Jennifer Papararo, Jon Sasaki, Cecilia Berkovic, Kate Monro and Emily Hogg, there were no clearly defined roles; there were simply a bunch of skills, aesthetics and experiments that everybody was involved in before, during and after any involvement with Instant Coffee. As much as we created work together, our individual work did not become meaningless if detached from Instant Coffee; it would just attract some other meaning. DeLanda cites Gilles Deleuze's theory of assemblages to account for these kinds of relations of exteriority, where 'part of an assemblage may be detached from it and plugged into a different assemblage in which its interactions are different.'[3]

This notion frees up the collaborators and leads to flexible, surprising results. Instant Coffee projects like, for example, Jon's BassBed, the subwoofer that also functioned as a bed, or Cecilia's Afghan blanket sculptures or even, for that matter, the listserv that Kate Monro maintains announcing other people's work, can all function easily on their own but, taken together as an assemblage, created a very flexible and dynamic collaborative environment and produced unexpected artistic products. My incorporation into the collective occurred because they liked my spin-the-bottle performance, swallowed it whole without diminishing any of my autonomy and seamlessly incorporated it into a series of their events, which became, for a moment, our events.

It's difficult to imagine applying this model to theatre, with its strict adherence to prefabricated scripts, hierarchical chains of command and narrowly defined roles, but the model offers insights that could pull us through to new and more contemporary and socially meaningful currents. Some Canadian artists seem to be experimenting with aspects of this approach, but a very clear example is Europe's Rimini Protocol. They often work with experts from a variety of other fields, building shows with these people, who collaborate as writers and performers. The individuals involved in their shows are not actors who, without lines to speak, become out-of-work actors, but are instead model-train enthusiasts, Indian call-centre

3 DeLanda, 10.

workers, female road construction workers – all of whom, when they are not in the show, retain their identity, continuing to do what they did all along. These are exciting ideas and theatre needs to incorporate them; the traditional well-made play process is so clearly and rapidly becoming an antiquated approach, unable to respond to contemporary social realities, while this model offers a way to incorporate current artistic developments: relational aesthetics, participation and civic engagement.

The final collaborative relationship, and a constant bane to the poor theatre practitioner, is that between the artist and the critic. There's something about the proximity of theatre – it's always a local experience – that often generates vitriolic bitchiness on the part of the critic. This is a symptom of narcissism of small differences. And maybe Canada, being, essentially, a small town masquerading as a country, generates a small-town criticism born simply of the embarrassment of being Canadian: not quite Europe, with all its state-subsidized culture, and not quite America, with its abundant private capital generating plenty of cultural innovation. No, we're Canada – middling state funding and a capitalist class no more interested in Canadian culture than is the beaver that is our symbol.

There are two schools of thought on the whole critic question: read 'em vs. avoid 'em. Many artists proudly assert their independence from the critical voice by claiming not to read them. But although criticism doesn't make it to my reading list when the subject is other people's work, when the show being reviewed is mine, I wake up at four in the morning to obsessively check the internet and then fire back a response while in as raw a state as possible. It's fun! Many people caution against this, claiming that kind of behaviour gives the critics too much power. But responding in a raw state is exactly what is demanded from a productive relationship. A frantic and anguished response is an honest one – why bother to take time to chill out and deal with things in a more level-headed way? When challenged by a collaborator in a rehearsal, working through the discomfort is the only way to go. Here too! And, like I said, it's fun. A raw, honest and even rude attack can generate a fruitful and productive antagonism.

Truthfully, it's been my experience that critics are rarely wrong in many of their specific criticisms; rather, they fail to consider wider contexts, other aspects or personal taste. This is no more apparent than when they're trying to deal with a silly show. And if you can say one thing about *[boxhead]*, it's that it's a fucking ridiculous show – thanks, again, to Alex Poch-Goldin. It's also confusing and thematically all over the map – my efforts to keep the meaning of the show beyond my grasp managed to hit the target.

I'll let critical collaborator Meg Walker, who reviewed the show for www.plankmagazine.com, explain, in a better way than I have never been able to, what the show is all about: 'Clearly, we humans are earnest in our desire for meaning, but also a bit silly in how far we'll take our explorations... [boxhead] lays out what's become a throughline to much of O'Donnell's work: if different divisions of "we" just talk to each other, we might actually like each other.'

Yeah, right, that's what I was trying to say. Thanks, Meg!

Darren O'Donnell

[boxhead]

Darren O'Donnell

for Paul Fauteux,
the original boxhead

Originally presented as a solo cabaret piece at Theatre Columbus's Mayhem and the Naked Muse in 1999, [boxhead] was first produced by Go-Chicken-Go at Factory Theatre in 2000, remounted at Theatre Passe Muraille in 2002 and then coproduced by Crow's Theatre and Mammalian Diving Reflex at the Magnetic North Theatre Festival in Vancouver and at Buddies in Bad Times in Toronto in 2008.

It has always been directed by Chris Abraham.

The original cast featured Paul Fauteux as Dr. Thoughtless Actions and Darren O'Donnell as Dr. Wishful Thinking, with Jim Jones stepping in to play Dr. Wishful Thinking in 2002 and Andrew Shaver and Adam Lazarus (Wishful and Thoughtless respectively) taking over in 2008.

The music was composed by Romano Di Nillo; set designed by Naomi Campbell, Darren O'Donnell and Chris Abraham; lighting designed by Steve Lucas with Sandra Marcroft; sound effects by Henry Monteforte and Tyler Devine and costumes by Nina Okens; production management by Trevor Schwellnus and orginally stage managed by the late, great Stephen Souter and subsequently by Beth Kates.

CHARACTERS

Dr. Thoughtless Actions, a young geneticist
Narrator Actions, an incorporeal being
Dr. Wishful Thinking, a young geneticist
Narrator Thinking, an incorporeal being

TIME

The year 8888.

STAGE

The set is pure black box, with curtains on either side, running upstage-downstage. Across the upstage border, curtains are also used to box things in. Behind the curtains on a platform stands the percussionist, whose hands, clad in white gloves and illuminated by black light, can be seen through a window in the otherwise solid black field. A scrim forms the fourth wall between the stage and the audience. A rope hangs on the audience side of the scrim, just to the side of the proscenium. A lit border frames the whole proscenium, mostly serving to mask the actors moving around in the dark, something they frequently do.

LIGHTS

We've always used nine top-lit spots, which reference petri dishes, arranged in a tic-tac-toe–like square on the whole stage, with other specials here and there. The lights, for the most part, function to isolate the actors in the space so that, as much as possible, they appear to be floating in darkness.

COSTUMES

Each doctor wears too-short beige polyester pants, a beige short-sleeve shirt, a brown bow-tie, black sneakers and a square brown box on his head. Dr. Thinking wears a purple lab coat and Dr. Actions wears an orange one.

SOUND EFFECTS

Two actors each play two characters. Their heads are in boxes, which also house microphones. The voices are channelled through an effects unit, creating the voices for the four characters. The doctors are pitched very high and the narrators very low. The effects are switched manually by a stage manager or sound operator.

MUSIC

The music is percussive and boxy, with real wooden boxes as instruments. There are also a few etheric sounds for more otherworldly moments.

PERFORMANCE STYLE

There are a lot of dumb jokes in the show and there is a fine line between making the joke and telegraphing that you are making the joke. Like pretty much all comedy, the actors should treat the absurd things that happen as seriously as Stanley howling for Stella. Physically, the challenge is to keep it as 'real' as possible, while still recognizing that extraordinary measures need to be taken in order to keep the audience staring at a couple of blank, expressionless beige surfaces.

SCENE ONE

NARRATOR ACTIONS: (*quietly and solemnly*) One morning, a young geneticist awoke to find a box had been secured to his head. It was a normal head, with typical accoutrements: eyes, ears, nose, mouth, hair and teeth – thirty-two of them.

The lights snap up to reveal Dr. Actions.

DR. ACTIONS: (*lifts his hands a little*) My god!

NARRATOR ACTIONS: The young geneticist was heard to cry, his first impression being that his eyes –

DR. ACTIONS: (*lifting his hands further*) My eyes!

NARRATOR ACTIONS: – had been glued shut.

DR. ACTIONS: Have been glued shut!

NARRATOR ACTIONS: (*returning his position to neutral*) Feeling the flutter of his panicked eyelashes against the inside of the intransigent box, the young geneticist reassessed his situation, coming to yet another incorrect conclusion:

DR. ACTIONS: Ohhhh! This must be a dream!

NARRATOR ACTIONS: And with this erroneous belief temporarily anchored in his fragile psyche, he proceeded to introduce himself to his dream:

DR. ACTIONS: Hello, I'd like to introduce myself to you, my dream ... but ... (*laughs awkwardly*) I'm in the embarrassing position of possessing a name that can't be pronounced due to the fact that it, and don't even try to think about it, is inconceivable. My name (*laughs awkwardly*) can't be conceived. The reason? Well, here it gets really messy and stupid and difficult to articulate but *(laughs)* the truth is my parents named me after words that burble just on the periphery of your consciousness in the third hour of lovemaking. You've heard them – you may not have noticed, but you have. So when you think of me, think of them, and, I must say, I have never met a dream I didn't like so, briefly, and according to the loose rules of social convention, *(he extends his hand)* it's nice to meet you.

NARRATOR ACTIONS: The young geneticist held his hand aloft waiting for the warm and humid clasp characteristic of the unconscious but found nothing but empty air.

DR. ACTIONS: *(extending his hand further)* It's nice to meet you.

NARRATOR ACTIONS: A cold sweat crawled its way from his perineum, up around the curve of his tiny bum, up into the small of his back, chilling its way to his shoulder blades, his neck, around his occiput, to the crown of his head and, pausing for a moment to catch its breath, the chill cascaded down the front of his body like a splashing bucket of crushed ice.

He retracts his hand with a sudden snap of fright.

DR. ACTIONS: *(he gasps)* I'm not dreaming!

NARRATOR ACTIONS: His penis suddenly shrunk, tightening in fright.

DR. ACTIONS: *(very panicked)* I'm awake.

NARRATOR ACTIONS: *(suddenly superdramatic)* And awake he was! Awake, terrified and finding himself, without a shadow of an indisputable doubt, utterly, undeniably, completely, thoroughly, uncompromisingly and unabashedly ... In! The! Dark!

DR. ACTIONS: *(right over the top like Gene Wilder in* Young Frankenstein*)* I'M! BLIND!

The lights crash to black.

NARRATOR ACTIONS: (*very quickly and even-metered, quietly as if spoken into the audience's ear but building, building, building as he goes*) Remember the morning when you were a child when you had a fever when your eyes infected when you awoke when you sat up when the pus of the people when eyelash to eyelash when no light would enter when it was dark when it was dark when it was dark!

The lights snap up.

DR. ACTIONS: Wait a fucking second! I'm not blind.(*His hands jump up to the sides of the box.*) I have a box on my head! (*Laughs in relief.*) I have a box on my head. I have a box on my head. (*He switches suddenly to serious realization.*) I have a box on my head! (*Then complete concern.*) I have a box on my head! (*Then complete panic, trying to yank it off.*) I have a box on my head! I have a box on my head. (*His body freezes.*)

NARRATOR ACTIONS: (*speaks slowly and sternly, almost patronizing*) Stay Calm, he thought to himself, Stay Calm. (*During the lines that follow, his arms slowly and cautiously lower to his thighs.*) There's nothing to worry about, it's only a box, after all; it's not the jaws of a crocodile, it's not the coils of a boa constrictor, it's not the uneasy feeling that America is really fucking it up this time that has gotten itself clamped around your big old head – it's just a box. A box.

A longish pause as the young geneticist contemplates the situation.

DR. ACTIONS: Hello?

NARRATOR ACTIONS: The young geneticist attempted a small foray of contact with the world at large.

DR. ACTIONS: Hello?

NARRATOR ACTIONS: He called to the ground.

DR. ACTIONS: Hello!?

NARRATOR ACTIONS: He called to the sky.

DR. ACTIONS: (*growing impatient*) Hello!?

NARRATOR ACTIONS: He called to the clouds that came in every shape he could imagine.

DR. ACTIONS: (*growing more impatient and insistent*) Hello! Hello!

NARRATOR ACTIONS: He called out his question to ugly, deaf heaven.

DR. ACTIONS: Hey! What's the big idea? Who's the wise guy that put the box onto my big fat old confused and butt-ugly head? Huh? What'd I ever do to you?

NARRATOR ACTIONS: What'd he ever do at all?

DR. ACTIONS: What'd I ever do to deserve this kinda fucking treatment?

NARRATOR ACTIONS: What the young geneticist didn't know was that, contrary to his understanding of the event as punitive, it was, in fact, for his own good. You see, on the back of box was written a word that addressed the young geneticist's state of affairs, explaining for one, all and everybody but him, the nature of his predicament, and that one word was (*whispers*) *fragile*.

DR. ACTIONS: (*The lights slowly fade throughout the course of his speech. Also, note that almost every sentence is a question and should be inflected upwards. Also, note that it turns into an evenly metered poem.*) What, what was that? Is there anybody there? Talk to me! Do you think I'm too ugly for the general public, for the common good? You think my gaze'll raze buildings? You think me Medusa? What gives? Is it me? No! I know your very problem: your hatred is focused on you, not me, and, perhaps do you somehow, think, somehow, you're undeserving, a kind of people for whom the little luxuries in life have been rightfully and lawfully withheld? A citizen without the ship? A ship without the state? You doubt your very sovereignty, your ability, your agility, you think you're floating stool? Upon the waves of life? You think you have no right? You think that you're unworthy of casting pernicious glances at my one and only, ohsoheavenly, absolutely fundamentally flawed and otherwise impeccable, now face the facts, delectable visage? My visawge? Perchance to chance a glance askance upon my royal nose and face and teeth and soul and looking straight at me you feel you will evaporate, launched laudably upon a sea of you and me and the words we hear in the absolute and deadening quiet when we wish upon eternity and hope that you're the you for me and I'm the me to set you free when the love is right and the world is wrong and we have soft and angry sex and watch the ticking clock its way for three hours long? (*in darkness*) Are you afraid?! Of the dark?!

The lights crash to black.

SCENE TWO

NARRATOR ACTIONS: One morning, a young geneticist awoke from a dream he could not remember, a dream in which he found that he was himself, a lonely god, floating aimlessly talking only to only itself.

Lights up.

DR. ACTIONS: I just had the strangest dream. Oh, I've forgotten it. Oh, no, I remember … oh wait. I just forgot again. Oh no, here it is! Oh, heck, it's gone again, I don't know what's wrong with me.

NARRATOR ACTIONS: One morning, a young geneticist awoke to find things were the same.

DR. ACTIONS: I think I remember a day before the box but why should I fixate on the immovable, the impossible, the impenetrable? May logic please grant me the whatever-it-takes to change the things I can and the whatever-it-takes to accept the things I can't.

NARRATOR ACTIONS: One morning, a young geneticist tried his best not to confuse the two.

DR. ACTIONS: The things I can change, the things I can't. The things I can change, the things I can't, the things I can change, the things I can't, the things I can change, the things I can't. (*freaking out*) How the heck can I tell the difference! Please, somebody, tell me what to do!

NARRATOR ACTIONS: One morning, a young geneticist awoke with a problem.

DR. ACTIONS: (*still freaking*) I could ask the tarot, or throw the I Ching, couldn't I? I could fart in the breeze and see what words form, I could scream against a wall, I could surf the internet clicking randomly from link to link to link, attempting to find something to tell me what to think. I could Google the word *meaning* and see what it found. Couldn't I? Couldn't I? Couldn't I? (*He folds his hands on his chest in childish frustration.*) The only thing I know how to change is my own diaper! Which is a good thing considering (*yells pointedly into the void*) there's no one else to do it!

Lights go to black.

DR. ACTIONS: Hey, who turned out the lights?

NARRATOR ACTIONS: One morning, a young geneticist awoke in a puddle of his own vomit.

Lights up.

DR. ACTIONS: I'm just a faceless, senseless, chattering smashfist, an urge to bust into pieces. I'm nothing. I'm no one. I don't have the strength to change a light bulb, let alone my life. I am a failure! A complete failure!

NARRATOR ACTIONS: One morning, a young geneticist decided to simply do his little best to end his little life.

DR. ACTIONS: Ladies and gentlemen who aren't even listening to me, who couldn't even care if I live or die, who don't even know I exist, well, fear not, in a moment what you already know will be true and I won't exist, so congratulations, way to go and thank you very much. Thank you for not even thinking of me once, even on today of all day of days, today: my birthday. Thank you for not buying me a present, or a cake, or providing a sickly candle upon which I could wish and blow, thank you for confirming what I already know: I don't exist, I'm not here, I haven't already went, I never was, so now I'll go. Goodbye and thank you very much, I'm spent, I'll relent, I'm not even here to pay the rent. And what better a day of day of days to end it all than the anniversary of the day upon which it all began, my birthday. Happy death day to me.

Perhaps modulating the voice in the middle of some of the words to reveal that it's the same actor playing both voices.

NARRATOR ACTIONS: (*singing*) Happy death day to you
      Happy death day to you
      Happy death day
      Happy death day
      Happy death day to –

DR. ACTIONS: – me.
    Well, here goes. (*He prepares to slit his wrists.*) I hope I don't get sprayed with blood.
    (*He hears something. A laugh, hopefully.*) Is there anybody there? Hello? I swear I heard something. Now where was I? Oh, right, of

course, suicide. (*He prepares to slit his wrist.*) Gosh, I hope the mayor comes to my funeral.

(*He hears something.*) Is there anybody there? I'm sure I heard a cough or a laugh or the sound of a bum shifting in a seat. Who's there? Hello, who's there. Hm, oh well. Now what was I doing? Oh, right, of course. (*He prepares to slit his wrist.*)

Wait a sec, have I changed my undies yet this year?

Who's there? Who's there? This is ridiculous. I'm trying to get some work done. (*He prepares to slit his wrist.*)

Oh geez, I hope nobody fucks my corpse ...

Dammit, dammit, dammit, who's there? This is ridiculous. There's nobody there. It's just me and my chattering brain. I can't concentrate. I can't focus long enough to kill myself. I'm too useless to even end my own stupid life. I'm a putrid utterly ridiculous nothing of a shitbag of a nobody. I'm a superduperpooperscooper, my own certified shit collector. I can't change the quality of my stupid experience here down here on lowly Planet Third ... but I can change the quantity! Eureka! That's it! That's it! I'm a geneticist, a young geneticist. I will inject a complete set of my DNA into the nucleus of another set of my DNA. If I can't change the quality of my life, I will change the quantity. My muscles will be bigger, my hands will be stronger, I'll have to duck through doorways. I will be huge! I will be huge! I will be huge! I will be twice the man I used to be. Well, here goes. Watch out world, here I come.

(*song, p. 116*) I'm feeling
good about life
I can
do anything
What's going to stand in my way?
Nothing!
Who's going to fuck up my plans?
No one!
Who's going to make love to me?
I am!

Who's going to tell me what to do?
Just me
Only me
Strictly me
Exclusively me
Undeniably independent out-of-this-world excellent
Me!

Blackout.

NARRATOR ACTIONS: One morning, a young geneticist decided to begin the experiment!

Lights up. Dr. Actions holds a syringe.

DR. ACTIONS: Oh boy, that looks like an awfully big needle. Well, here goes. (*He sticks it into one side of his box and withdraws his DNA.*) Ahhhhhhh! (*He pulls it out.*)

Aw, there's my DNA. Shake it up. (*He shakes up his DNA.*) Say goodbye to little ol' little ol' me. (*He sticks it into the other side of his box and injects himself.*) Ahhhhhhhh! (*He pulls it out.*) Whew, that wasn't so bad. (*He waits, looks at his hands, looks at his feet, waits. Nothing happens.*)

Nothing.

He is suddenly gripped by agony. He bounces and flails around the stage as the lights flicker. Suddenly, an additional arm appears, another arm, two legs and a head. The two men peel apart and collapse to the floor, unaware of each other.

BOTH DOCTORS: I'm just me, me and only me. What a

DR. THINKING: beautiful

DR. ACTIONS: rotten

BOTH DOCTORS: thing to be on this day of special special day of days,

DR. ACTIONS: my one and only

DR. THINKING: just me lonely

DR. ACTIONS: happy

DR. THINKING: dippy

DR. ACTIONS: dipple

DR. THINKING: dappy,

BOTH DOCTORS: my happy ever hopeful after,

DR. THINKING: hold your breath,

DR. ACTIONS: hold the laughter – sad and angry daily prayer –

DR. THINKING: dedicated to the boy and girls down here

DR. ACTIONS: on the horrified appearance of my single

DR. THINKING: bloody

DR. ACTIONS: beady

DR. THINKING: eye

DR. ACTIONS: on this scorched plain,

BOTH DOCTORS: this super-exploitation station, down low on lowly Planet Third,

DR. THINKING: the one and only day of days,

DR. ACTIONS: the day to celebrate the beginning of my birth

BOTH DOCTORS: on Earth

DR. ACTIONS: in short

DR. THINKING: and simply

DR. ACTIONS: simple

DR. THINKING: said

BOTH DOCTORS: the day I cease to be the dead

DR. ACTIONS: and woke

DR. THINKING: and coughed

DR. ACTIONS: and squawked

DR. THINKING: and reminded all who try to duck,

BOTH DOCTORS: well, fuck, it's my birthday!

DR. THINKING: It's my birthday!

DR. ACTIONS: It's my birthday!

DR. THINKING: It's my birthday!

DR. ACTIONS: It's my birthday!

DR. THINKING: It's my birthday!

DR. ACTIONS: It's my birthday!

NARRATOR THINKING: It's my birthday.

Blackout.

SCENE THREE

NARRATOR ACTIONS: One morning, an excited young geneticist with a box on his head acted without the intrusive hindrance of thought.

Lights up.

DR. ACTIONS: Hey, everybody, watch me take a poop with my mouth!

Lights out.

NARRATOR ACTIONS: His friends called him Thoughtless.

NARRATOR THINKING: One morning, an excited young geneticist with a box on his head based all his thoughts on the thin wisps of wishes.

Lights up.

DR. THINKING: Hey, everybody, think about it: poop doesn't have to taste bad – it's a matter of how you look at it.

Lights out.

NARRATOR THINKING: His friends called him Wishful.

NARRATOR ACTIONS: One morning, Dr. Thoughtless Actions, Scientific Applicator and perpetrator of theories relating to acting within the confines of a box, awoke in his hotel room at the International Conference of Things Come Together to find a box still secured to his head.

Lights up.

DR. ACTIONS: Oh, for fuck's sake!

Lights out.

NARRATOR THINKING: One morning, Dr. Wishful Thinking, Scientific Applicator and perpetrator of theories relating to thinking within the confines of a box, awoke in his hotel room at the International Conference of Things Come Undone to find a box still secured to his head.

Lights up.

DR. THINKING: Oh, for fuck's sake!

Lights out.

NARRATOR ACTIONS: The box blocked the light.

NARRATOR THINKING: The box blocked the light.

Lights up.

DR. ACTIONS: Great! This is just fucking great. I'm supposed to be presenting my research paper, 'How You Too Can Act Happily Within The Confines of a Box,' to the Academy of Things Come Together and I still can't see a fucking thing!

DR. THINKING: Great! This is just fucking great. I'm supposed to be presenting my research paper, 'How You Too Can Think Happily Within the Confines of a Box,' to the Academy of Things Come Undone and I still can't see a fucking thing!

NARRATOR ACTIONS: Dr. Thoughtless Actions, world famous for making mistakes, decided to leap to the wrong conclusion.

NARRATOR THINKING: Dr. Wishful Thinking, world famous for missing the point, decided to rub things the wrong way.

NARRATOR ACTIONS: We're going to leap to the wrong conclusion.

NARRATOR THINKING: We're going to rub things the wrong way.

NARRATOR ACTIONS: I said we're going leap to a wrong conclusion.

NARRATOR THINKING: I said we're going to rub things the wrong way.

Pause.

NARRATOR ACTIONS: You know, though I as narrator possess no body, have no head, am, in fact, a member of Team Incorporeal, I swear I heard another voice reverberating in my not-really-there cranium.

NARRATOR THINKING: You know, I just experienced the illusion that my narratorness has developed a small doppelgängster who was brazen enough to somehow refer to me as a mere echo, a contingent and unimportant reverberatory fictive notion.

NARRATOR ACTIONS: Perhaps there's the small chance that Dr. Thoughtless Actions can account for this phenomenomenology. Oh, Doctor!

DR. ACTIONS: Say, I'm experiencing what the mystics refer to as a voice in my head.

NARRATOR THINKING: Dr. Thinking, Dr. Thinking, paging Dr. Thinking.

DR. THINKING: Say, is that a vocal hallucination or am I just hearing voices?

NARRATOR THINKING: Dr. Thinking –

DR. THINKING: You can call me Wishful.

NARRATOR ACTIONS: Dr. Actions –

DR. ACTIONS: You can call me Thoughtless.

NARRATOR THINKING: Doctor, I seem to be in the

NARRATOR ACTIONS: embarrassing position of,

NARRATOR THINKING: well, heh, heh, it is rather

NARRATOR ACTIONS: difficult to describe but,

NARRATOR THINKING: well, let me start from

NARRATOR ACTIONS: the beginningish, I guess.

NARRATOR THINKING: I always held as a reassuring certainty the opinion

NARRATOR ACTIONS: that I was, like it or not,

NARRATOR THINKING: alone

NARRATOR ACTIONS: in the universe.

BOTH DOCTORS: And now?

NARRATOR THINKING: Well, around the time you discovered the box on
  your head –

BOTH DOCTORS: Oh, right, right, that's what this is.

NARRATOR ACTIONS: Well,

NARRATOR THINKING: since then,

NARRATOR ACTIONS: I've sensed the presence of some

NARRATOR THINKING: one

NARRATOR ACTIONS: thing

NARRATOR THINKING: else.

NARRATOR ACTIONS: It's got me

NARRATOR THINKING: all up in a tizzy.

Pause.

DR. ACTIONS: Well,

DR. THINKING: you know,

BOTH DOCTORS: I'm not a psychiatrist, I'm a Geneticist Spectacular Mind Holography Consultant Expert.

NARRATOR ACTIONS: Well, yes,

NARRATOR THINKING: sir,

NARRATOR ACTIONS: I'm aware of that.

BOTH DOCTORS: Please, please, don't call me sir.

NARRATOR THINKING: I was hoping

NARRATOR ACTIONS: that you might

NARRATOR THINKING: be able to supply

NARRATOR ACTIONS: a theoretical foundation

NARRATOR THINKING: to this sinking feeling

NARRATOR ACTIONS: I've been having

NARRATOR THINKING: that I'm not

BOTH NARRATORS: alone.

DR. ACTIONS: Well, let me share a little of my recent discoveries with you.

DR. THINKING: Well, let me share a little of my recent discoveries with you.

NARRATOR ACTIONS: Ladies and gentlemen,

At the same time.
NARRATOR ACTIONS: Dr. Wishful Actions.
NARRATOR THINKING: Dr. Thoughtful Thinking.

DR. ACTIONS: Thank you very much.

DR. THINKING: Thank you very much.

DR. ACTIONS: The problem with doing things yourself

DR. THINKING: The problem with doing things yourself

DR. ACTIONS: in the face of

DR. THINKING: in light of

BOTH DOCTORS: getting them done

DR. ACTIONS: is the fact that, woven in your idea of me

DR. THINKING: is your idea of you.

DR. ACTIONS: And woven in your idea of you

DR. THINKING: is your idea of me.

DR. ACTIONS: Not me myself,

DR. THINKING: but you yourself,

DR. ACTIONS: not something else,

DR. THINKING: you yourself,

DR. ACTIONS: you through me.

DR. THINKING: Not me myself,

DR. ACTIONS: but your idea

DR. THINKING: your idea of me.

DR. ACTIONS: You.

DR. THINKING: You.

BOTH DOCTORS: And only you.

DR. ACTIONS: And you

DR. THINKING: And you

DR. ACTIONS: are in

DR. THINKING: are in

BOTH DOCTORS: control.

DR. ACTIONS: So my advice to you is

DR. THINKING: ignore the voices in your head,

DR. ACTIONS: enjoy life to the fullest

DR. THINKING: and simply try your best to

BOTH DOCTORS: Think. Outside. The box.

BOTH NARRATORS: Why, thank you very much, Doctor.

DR. ACTIONS: You're welcome.

DR. THINKING: My pleasure.

They hear each other for the first time.

DR. ACTIONS: You're pleasure?

DR. THINKING: My welcome?

BOTH NARRATORS: The doctor, Dr.

NARRATOR ACTIONS: Thoughtless

NARRATOR THINKING: Wishful

NARRATOR ACTIONS: Actions

NARRATOR THINKING: Thinking paused,

NARRATOR ACTIONS: felt something was slightly awry,

NARRATOR THINKING: and listened,

NARRATOR ACTIONS: attempting to hear past the box.

DR. THINKING: I have this

DR. ACTIONS: sneaking suspicion

DR. THINKING: that

DR. ACTIONS: someone

DR. THINKING: is

DR. ACTIONS: finishing.

DR. THINKING: my

DR. ACTIONS: sentences?

DR. THINKING: Exactly, my

DR. ACTIONS: sentences.

NARRATOR ACTIONS: That's

NARRATOR THINKING: what

NARRATOR ACTIONS: I

NARRATOR THINKING: was

NARRATOR ACTIONS: trying

NARRATOR THINKING: to

NARRATOR ACTIONS: tell

NARRATOR THINKING: you!

BOTH DOCTORS: My god, there is somebody else here!

Pause.

DR. THINKING: (*tentatively*) Hello?

DR. ACTIONS: Hi.

DR. THINKING: Who are you?

DR. ACTIONS: Actions, Dr. Thoughtless Actions.

DR. THINKING: Pleased to meet you. I'm Thinking, Dr. Wishful Thinking.

DR. ACTIONS: Pleased to meet you. Are you lecturing tonight?

DR. THINKING: I was under the impression I was lecturing right now.

DR. ACTIONS: Really, I seem to have been suffering a similar delusion.

DR. THINKING: I was wondering if you could tell me

DR. ACTIONS: I was hoping you might be able to shed light on

BOTH DOCTORS: whether or not there appears to be a box on my mind!

BOTH DOCTORS: What?

BOTH DOCTORS: I'm sorry, what did you say?

BOTH DOCTORS: I'm having trouble hearing you.

BOTH DOCTORS: Did you say there was a box on my mind?

BOTH DOCTORS: Dammit, I swear there was somebody there!

NARRATOR ACTIONS: And from that point on

NARRATOR THINKING: And from that point on

NARRATOR ACTIONS: Dr. Thoughtless Actions

NARRATOR THINKING: Dr. Wishful Thinking

NARRATOR ACTIONS: withdrew

NARRATOR THINKING: withdrew

NARRATOR ACTIONS: from his research

NARRATOR THINKING: from his research

NARRATOR ACTIONS: on living happily

NARRATOR THINKING: on living happily

NARRATOR ACTIONS: within the confines

NARRATOR THINKING: within the confines

NARRATOR ACTIONS: of the box

NARRATOR THINKING: of the box

NARRATOR ACTIONS: and instead

NARRATOR THINKING: and instead

NARRATOR ACTIONS: focused

NARRATOR THINKING: focused

NARRATOR ACTIONS: his research

NARRATOR THINKING: his research

BOTH NARRATORS: on echoes

BOTH DOCTORS: on echoes?

BOTH NARRATORS: On echoes.

BOTH DOCTORS: On echoes?

BOTH NARRATORS: (*very firmly*) On echoes.

BOTH DOCTORS: (*reluctantly*) On ... echoes.

BOTH NARRATORS: Echoes.

BOTH DOCTORS: Echoes.

Blackout.

SCENE FOUR

The stage remains in darkness.

NARRATOR THINKING: Have you been his narrator for long?

NARRATOR ACTIONS: Well, I used to be considered a god.

NARRATOR THINKING: (*chuckles*) Man, those were the days.

NARRATOR ACTIONS: You're telling me.

NARRATOR THINKING: Back before the corpus collosum.

NARRATOR ACTIONS: Yup, back in the days of monotheism.

NARRATOR THINKING: Back when the universe was rational.

NARRATOR THINKING: God, I crave that.

NARRATOR THINKING: I feel my omniscience ebbing away.

NARRATOR ACTIONS: I used to think I knew everything.

NARRATOR THINKING: I remember that feeling.

NARRATOR ACTIONS: Now the only thing of which I'm certain is uncertainty.

NARRATOR THINKING: Change is the only constant, babe.

NARRATOR ACTIONS: I'm scared.

NARRATOR THINKING: Things will turn around.

NARRATOR ACTIONS: I don't know that.

NARRATOR THINKING: You've got to have faith.

NARRATOR ACTIONS: In what?

NARRATOR THINKING: Yourself.

NARRATOR ACTIONS: Even when nobody else does?

NARRATOR THINKING: Especially when nobody else does.

Pause.

NARRATOR ACTIONS: I love you.

NARRATOR THINKING: You don't have to say that.

NARRATOR ACTIONS: I know.

NARRATOR THINKING: You don't really know me.

NARRATOR ACTIONS: Aw, I know enough about you – you're the same as me. We're just two voices without heads.

Pause.

NARRATOR THINKING: Kiss me.

NARRATOR ACTIONS: But we don't have lips.

NARRATOR THINKING: Oh, right.

SCENE FIVE

Lights up. The two doctors stand as if delivering a speech to a rapt audience. Perhaps they stand facing upstage.

DR. ACTIONS: The echo:

DR. THINKING: The echo is a phenomenon

DR. ACTIONS: though believed to be understood

DR. THINKING: by the mainstream of science,

DR. ACTIONS: is still held by radical science

DR. THINKING: as yet possessing a mystery impenetrable.

DR. ACTIONS: Like the still-living light from a distant star already long since dead,

DR. THINKING: the sound of your own voice bounces back and makes you think of yourself

BOTH DOCTORS: twice.

DR. THINKING: (*flips suddenly into a petulant rage as if the previous address were merely for the benefit of the mirror*) And I'm sick of thinking about myself twice!

DR. ACTIONS: (*does the same*) I don't even want to think of myself once!

DR. THINKING: There was a day I thought somebody was there.

DR. ACTIONS: But I was wrong wrong wrong!

DR. THINKING: I'm isolated in this stupid box listening to my voice bouncing back and slapping me in the face!

DR. ACTIONS: Everything I hear sounds like an echo of everything else!

DR. THINKING: And, frankly, beyond the obvious annoyance of hearing everything twice, it's got me constantly craving some form of companionship!

DR. ACTIONS: It's a nefariously subtle teasing mechanism tempting me with an unachievable simpatico.

DR. THINKING: For imagine if the echo were truly alive and I could talk to myself – oh, what a glorious day that would be!

DR. ACTIONS: But, alas, an echo is a lie, a ruse, a no-one, a no-how, a no-show, a know-nothing.

DR. THINKING: This deceit must stop.

DR. ACTIONS: I must deprive myself of this phony friendship.

DR. THINKING: I will toil away until the day I create ...

DR. ACTIONS: The echoless yell.

DR. THINKING: The echoless yell.

DR. ACTIONS: The echoless yell.

DR. THINKING: The echoless yell!

DR. ACTIONS: The echoless yell!

DR. THINKING: The echoless yell.

DR. ACTIONS: The echoless yell.

DR. THINKING: The echoless yell!

DR. ACTIONS: The echoless yell!

Blackout.

NARRATOR THINKING: I once fashioned a bicycle from the foam of my thoughts and I rode in what can best be described as circles looking for a party I might have read about on the internet hoping for something that could be referred to as friendship.

Lights slowly rising to reveal the two doctors standing face to face. They lift their hands up and touch as if looking into a mirror.

NARRATOR ACTIONS: I was peeking over my own shoulder watching myself encounter myself. It was a beautiful day. It was back before the big bang, back before the inflationary era, even back before I'd had a hope in hell.

NARRATOR THINKING: I always had this sneaking suspicion that there are parts of me that know me so much more than the rest of me. And those parts keep me in the dark. Not because I'm too weak to sustain the truth but because a divided self is simply less lonely.

DR. ACTIONS: And I am so

DR. THINKING: And I'm so

DR. ACTIONS: lonely.

DR. THINKING: lonely.

Lights out.

NARRATOR ACTIONS: Lonely.

NARRATOR THINKING: Lonely.

SCENE SIX

BOTH NARRATORS: One morning,

NARRATOR ACTIONS: Oh, sorry.

NARRATOR THINKING: It's all right, you go.

NARRATOR ACTIONS: No, it's okay, after you.

NARRATOR THINKING: No, really, I'm in no rush.

NARRATOR ACTIONS: Seriously.

NARRATOR THINKING: No, no –

BOTH NARRATORS: One morning (*They both laugh.*)

NARRATOR ACTIONS: You go!

NARRATOR THINKING: Really, after you.

BOTH NARRATORS: One morning (*They both laugh uproariously.*)

NARRATOR ACTIONS: Okay, let's do this alphabetically.

NARRATOR THINKING: Good idea.

NARRATOR ACTIONS: What's your name?

NARRATOR THINKING: Oh, uh, my name. Uh, what's yours?

NARRATOR ACTIONS: Oh, my name is, uh, well, it's a little embarrassing, but it

BOTH NARRATORS: can't be conceived? (*They laugh again.*)

NARRATOR THINKING: Neither can mine.

NARRATOR ACTIONS: Well, let's just refer to each other in the fourth person.

NARRATOR THINKING: One morning, Dr. Wishful Thinking walked to a nearby canyon to test his new invention, the Echoless Yell.

Lights up.

DR. THINKING: Hello!

Lights out.

NARRATOR ACTIONS: One morning, Dr. Thoughtless Actions walked to a nearby canyon to test his new invention, the Echoless Yell.

Lights up.

DR. ACTIONS: Hello!

Lights out.

NARRATOR THINKING: Dr. Thinking, hearing the voice of Dr. Actions and thinking his efforts had failed, tried again.

Lights up.

DR. THINKING: Hello!

Lights out.

NARRATOR ACTIONS: Dr. Actions, hearing the voice of Dr. Thinking, and acting on his feeling that his efforts had failed, tried again.

Lights up.

DR. ACTIONS: Hello!

DR. THINKING: Dammit, in the laboratory my yell was echoless. Hello!

DR. ACTIONS: This is a ludicrous! That yell was designed to be without peer, independent and alone. Hello!

DR. THINKING: Well, once again, failure and obscurity is my fate. I'm, frankly, getting used to it.

NARRATOR THINKING: Dr. Thinking, having abandoned the project, allowed Dr. Actions' last yell to hang without a reply. Dr. Actions had succeeded.

DR. ACTIONS: Eureka! I've succeeded!

DR. THINKING: Eureka? I've succeeded?

DR. ACTIONS: Or have I failed? Eureka?

DR. THINKING: Eureka?

DR. ACTIONS: I have failed.

DR. THINKING: Where does this *eureka* originate? Have I discovered another dimension?

DR. ACTIONS: I am a foolish stupid scientist fading into nothingness. I curse myself: damn you, Dr. Actions!

DR. THINKING: Dr. Actions? But I'm Dr. Thinking!

DR. ACTIONS: Dr. Thinking? But I'm Dr. Actions!

DR. THINKING: Dr. Actions, Dr. Thoughtless Actions?

DR. ACTIONS: The same. And you are?

DR. THINKING: Thinking, Dr. Wishful Thinking.

DR. ACTIONS: That sounds familiar.

DR. THINKING: I do believe we've met.

DR. ACTIONS: Yes! At the International Conference of

At the same time.

DR. ACTIONS: Things Come Together!
DR. THINKING: Things Come Undone!

DR. ACTIONS: Things Come Undone!
DR. THINKING: Things Come Together!

DR. ACTIONS: Things Come Together!
DR. THINKING: Things Come Undone!

DR. ACTIONS: That's right!

DR. THINKING: I always thought you were a figment of my imagination.

DR. ACTIONS: Imagine that, so did I.

DR. THINKING: You thought you were a figment of my imagination? That's incredible!

DR. ACTIONS: No, no, I thought you were a figment of my imagination, you silly man.

DR. THINKING: I was only trying to be charming.

DR. ACTIONS: Well, mission accomplished, squarehead.

DR. THINKING: And I return the compliment.

DR. ACTIONS: Compliment accepted.

NARRATOR THINKING: They seem to be getting along fine.

NARRATOR ACTIONS: Yes, they do.

NARRATOR THINKING: Without us, I mean.

DR. ACTIONS: Perhaps you'd like to drop by my lab and take a look at some of my work – I've got one echo that's been trapped in a vial for a year now.

DR. THINKING: Incredible – as do I!

DR. ACTIONS: Synchrondipity! What's the content of your echo?

DR. THINKING: It's just a simple three-word sentence!

DR. ACTIONS: Truly amazing. Mine's a mere simple three-word sentence as well.

DR. THINKING: This is getting uncanny!

DR. ACTIONS: I'm almost afraid to ask what the content of your sentence is.

DR. THINKING: I'm feeling a similarly chilling apprehension.

DR. ACTIONS: For if they were identical –

DR. THINKING: God forbid.

NARRATOR ACTIONS: Why would I forbid it, for god's sake?

NARRATOR THINKING: For my sake?

DR. ACTIONS: If they were identical,

DR. THINKING: with that many coincidences in one afternoon,

DR. ACTIONS: I would have to reconcieve my conception

DR. THINKING: of the universe.

BOTH DOCTORS: And I'm not going to do that.

DR. THINKING: But what if they are the same?

DR. ACTIONS: If they are the same.

DR. THINKING: And we're forced to reconceive our conception of the universe?

DR. ACTIONS: If they are the same, we must deny the evidence, believe what we've always believed, part and never speak again, agreed?

DR. THINKING: Agreed. (He *extends his hand to shake. They have a short shtick trying to locate the other's hand. They shake.*)

BOTH DOCTORS: The sentence is – (*They laugh.*)

DR. ACTIONS: After you.

DR. THINKING: No, no, after you.

DR. ACTIONS: No, really.

DR. THINKING: I insist.

BOTH DOCTORS: The sentence is – (*They laugh again, louder.*)

DR. ACTIONS: Shall we go alphabetically?

DR. THINKING: Good idea.

BOTH DOCTORS: The sentence is – (*They laugh.*)

DR. THINKING: Are we using our first or last name?

DR. ACTIONS: But both *Thoughtless* and *Actions* come before *Wishful* and *Thinking.*

DR. THINKING: I was going by your first name and my last name, in which case, I would be first.

DR. ACTIONS: Why don't we just go by our last names?

DR. THINKING: In which case?

DR. ACTIONS: Well, Actions always come before Thinking.

DR. THINKING: As they should.

DR. ACTIONS: Therefore, after me.

DR. THINKING: Take it away.

DR. ACTIONS: The sentence I have trapped echoing in my vial is ...

DR. THINKING: Is?

DR. ACTIONS: Is ...

DR. THINKING: Is?

DR. ACTIONS: Is ...

DR. THINKING: Is?

DR. ACTIONS: Is: *I love you.*

DR. THINKING: Whew, that's a relief. No synchrondipitous overkill here.

DR. ACTIONS: That's good news! So, what's the sentence echoing in your vial?

DR. THINKING: It's not even related.

DR. ACTIONS: But in the pursuit of scientific knowledge?

DR. THINKING: All right. It's: *I hate you.*

DR. ACTIONS: Oh, you're on a whole other path. Thank goodness.

NARRATOR THINKING: You mean thank god, don't you?

DR. THINKING: Perhaps our research could complement each other.

DR. ACTIONS: Ideal.

DR. THINKING: Shall I come up to your lab?

DR. ACTIONS: Just what I was thinking, Dr. Thinking.

DR. THINKING: Just what I thought.

Snap to black.

SCENE SEVEN

NARRATOR THINKING: 'Thank goodness'? He said, 'Thank goodness.'

NARRATOR ACTIONS: So they're getting on without us.

NARRATOR THINKING: That's an understatement.

NARRATOR ACTIONS: Well, what's the problem?

NARRATOR THINKING: I was having trouble jumping in to narrate the action.

NARRATOR ACTIONS: Why didn't you just watch?

NARRATOR THINKING: It's difficult for me to formulate a sense of purpose in such a passive state.

NARRATOR ACTIONS: Even if watching is your purpose?

NARRATOR THINKING: Oh great, from a vengeful god to a watchful god. Sounds like a demotion to me.

NARRATOR ACTIONS: Nobody thinks we're gods anymore. It's over, don't you get it?

NARRATOR THINKING: All right, from an omniscient narrator to a narrator who doesn't know shit. That's a fucking demotion.

NARRATOR ACTIONS: Do you have to know everything?

NARRATOR THINKING: I don't have to know everything. I would just like to feel needed, like my input is appreciated.

NARRATOR ACTIONS: I appreciate you. I've always appreciated you.

NARRATOR THINKING: You appreciate my company. I don't provide any meaning to your life.

NARRATOR ACTIONS: But you do for them.

Lights up on audience.

NARRATOR THINKING: Do I?

NARRATOR ACTIONS: Sure, we both do.

NARRATOR THINKING: Really?

NARRATOR ACTIONS: Sure, watch. (*Lights out on audience.*)
One morning, Drs. Thinking and Actions awoke on a beautiful beach on a distant planet in a tropical paradise.

Lights up.

DR. THINKING: Wow! The weather's great! Let's go for a swim.

DR. ACTIONS: Last one in the water's a sphere!

Blackout.

NARRATOR ACTIONS: See, we create location just by simple suggestion. We're very powerful. Without us, the audience has no idea where those boxheaded morons are.

NARRATOR THINKING: Are you saying we signify space?

NARRATOR ACTIONS: We *are* space.

NARRATOR THINKING: Let me try. One morning, Drs. Actions and Thinking awoke floating in space.

Lights up to reveal the two doctors floating in space.

DR. ACTIONS: Whoooooaaahhhh!

DR. THINKING: Who took the Earth?

Blackout.

NARRATOR THINKING: That's very cool.

NARRATOR ACTIONS: See. Feeling better?

NARRATOR THINKING: A little, but, honestly, I feel neglected.

NARRATOR ACTIONS: Well, here, let me give you a back rub.

NARRATOR THINKING: But I don't have a back.

NARRATOR ACTIONS: Oh, right.

SCENE EIGHT

NARRATOR THINKING: One morning, after a restless night, Drs. Thinking

NARRATOR ACTIONS: and Actions convened at the lab to continue their research on

Lights up.

DR. THINKING: No, we're not going to do that.

NARRATOR THINKING: I'm sorry?

DR. THINKING: We're not doing that.

NARRATOR ACTIONS: Not doing what, sweetie?

DR. THINKING: We're not going to study echoes. We're going to study this box. We're going to take it apart, we're going to check it out and we're going to get it the fuck off our heads.

NARRATOR THINKING: One morning, after a restless night, Drs. Thinking and

DR. THINKING: No, that's it for mornings. Okay, no more mornings, I've had it. (*starts to get hysterical*) We've got to get this goddamn box off. I can't believe this! I've lost track of how long we've had these things on our stupid fucking

DR. ACTIONS: Just, whatever, calm down.

DR. THINKING: You calm down.

DR. ACTIONS: Just do what he says.

DR. THINKING: You do what he says.

DR. ACTIONS: Look, it'll probably be fun.

Pause.

DR. THINKING: Fuck fun.

NARRATOR THINKING: (*sighs with some animosity*) One morning, Drs. Thinking

NARRATOR ACTIONS: and Actions convened at the lab.

Lights up.

DR. THINKING: I had the craziest dream, okay? You happy?

DR. ACTIONS: Synchrondipity!

DR. THINKING: (*under his breath*) Yeah, synchrondipity all right. (*aloud*) I dreamt that we were floating somewhere in a vast array of space.

DR. ACTIONS: Beautiful!

DR. THINKING: It was terrifying, actually.

DR. ACTIONS: I dreamt that we found ourselves on a planet of tropical origins basking in the blaze of six suns: two rising, one setting, one at midday and two eclipsed by the two of twenty-three moons that revolved around our spinning heads.

DR. THINKING: Beautiful!

DR. ACTIONS: What do you think it all means?

DR. THINKING: I think it means that our collaboration is destined for great heights and the basking glory of interplanetary fame and fortune.

DR. ACTIONS: But you said your dream was terrifying.

DR. THINKING: Well, I've always been afraid of success.

DR. ACTIONS: Well, get over it, Blockbrain. Now that we've invented the Echoless Yell, nothing is going to get in our way. Lay it on me.

DR. THINKING: I love you!

DR. ACTIONS: Beautiful.

DR. THINKING: Sublime.

DR. ACTIONS: Now that we've created a yell without peer,

DR. THINKING: a yell that lives alone,

DR. ACTIONS: a yell without the little buddy of a little echo,

DR. THINKING: we must together create an echo that doesn't need to bounce back.

DR. ACTIONS: That's brilliant! An echo with no need to go nowhere.

DR. THINKING: That's brilliant! An echo that erupts spontaneously on the spot.

DR. ACTIONS: That's brilliant. An echo that doesn't require space!

DR. THINKING: That's brilliant! (*song, p. 117*) You're brilliant

DR. ACTIONS: Thank you for noticing, but
(*singing*) You're brilliant

DR. THINKING: I've always suspected, but
(*singing*) You're brilliant

DR. ACTIONS: Can I put that on my resume?
(*singing*) You're brilliant

DR. THINKING: I'll carve that on my tombstone
(*singing*) You're brilliant

DR. ACTIONS: (*singing*) You're brilliant for thinking I'm brilliant.

DR. THINKING: (*singing*) You're brilliant for thinking I'm brilliant for thinking you're brilliant.

DR. ACTIONS: (*singing*) You're brilliant for thinking I'm brilliant for thinking you're brilliant for thinking I'm brilliant.

BOTH DOCTORS: (*singing*) Brilliant!
        Brilliant!

        The world will adore us, they'll think that we are great
        No one else compares, no one else will rate
        We're the smartest in the solar system, glory is our fate
        The world will must obey us, they mustn't hesitate
        Or it will be too late

        You're brilliant
        You're brilliant

DR. ACTIONS: You're brilliant for thinking I'm brilliant.

DR. THINKING: You're brilliant for thinking I'm brilliant for thinking you're brilliant.

DR. ACTIONS: You're brilliant for thinking I'm brilliant for thinking you're brilliant for thinking I'm brilliant.

BOTH DOCTORS: (*They get a little too much into their song.*) You're brilliant for thinking I'm brilliant for thinking (etc. etc.!)

NARRATOR THINKING: Cut it, cut it already!

Lights out.

NARRATOR ACTIONS: They're fine.

NARRATOR THINKING: They're not fine, they're losing their marbles.

NARRATOR ACTIONS: Anyway, the doctors

NARRATOR THINKING: We've got to be careful.

NARRATOR ACTIONS: The doctors

NARRATOR THINKING: (*sighs*) Thinking

NARRATOR ACTIONS: and Actions

NARRATOR THINKING: focused their entire attention on the duplication of an echo, applying certain techniques involving

NARRATOR ACTIONS: petri dishes

NARRATOR THINKING: and agar.

Lights up. The doctors are yelling into petri dishes.

DR. ACTIONS: Yell louder.

DR. THINKING: I love you!

DR. ACTIONS: Nice one. Here. (*passes him another petri dish*) Try a whisper.

DR. THINKING: I hate you!

Lights out.

NARRATOR ACTIONS: The doctors

NARRATOR THINKING: Thinking

NARRATOR ACTIONS: and Actions

NARRATOR THINKING: worked feverishly,

NARRATOR ACTIONS: day in day out,

NARRATOR THINKING: Attempting to clone a yell.

Lights up.

DR. ACTIONS: Try it in French.

DR. THINKING: Je t'aime!

DR. ACTIONS: Nice.

DR. THINKING: How are yesterday's sounding?

Dr. Actions lifts a few petri dishes and holds them to the side of his box.

DR. ACTIONS: I don't hear a thing.

DR. THINKING: It's still early.

NARRATOR ACTIONS: The doctors

NARRATOR THINKING: Thinking

NARRATOR ACTIONS: and Actions

NARRATOR THINKING: decided to crank up the heat.

DR. ACTIONS: Perhaps the temperature in here is not conducive.

DR. THINKING: We could do something to fix that.

DR. ACTIONS: Like what?

DR. THINKING: Well, as a scientist dedicated to whatever it takes, I propose friction.

DR. ACTIONS: So, kiss me.

DR. THINKING: Just the action I was thinking, Dr. Actions.

DR. ACTIONS: And that's the kind of thinking we need to act on, Dr. Thinking.

They start to make out passionately.

DR. THINKING: I want you; I've wanted you since the day I thought you were a figment of my imagination.

DR. ACTIONS: Synchrondipitous.

DR. THINKING: You too?

DR. ACTIONS: There's something about you that's so familiar.

DR. THINKING: I feel like I've known you all my life.

DR. ACTIONS: I feel like we're two cubes squared.

DR. THINKING: I feel like you know all the punchlines to my jokes.

DR. ACTIONS: I feel like I can

DR. THINKING: read my mind?

DR. ACTIONS: No, not that.

DR. THINKING: Well, let me read my mind for you: take me home, Dr. Actions, and make me rectangular!

They go at it ferociously.

Fade to black.

SCENE NINE

NARRATOR ACTIONS: The two doctors

NARRATOR THINKING: Thinking

NARRATOR ACTIONS: and Actions,

NARRATOR THINKING: taking a short break from their research on echoes,

NARRATOR ACTIONS: began to dabble in the words that burble on the periphery of your consciousness in the third hour of fucking.

NARRATOR THINKING: You know the ones.

NARRATOR ACTIONS: You've heard them.

NARRATOR THINKING: Your attention may have been elsewhere,

NARRATOR ACTIONS: it being the act of fucking,

NARRATOR THINKING: but you've heard them.

NARRATOR ACTIONS: You have, you really have.

NARRATOR THINKING: They sound something like this:

NARRATOR ACTIONS: (*song, p. 122*) Do do do-do
     Do-do do
     Do-do-do do-do do-do do

NARRATOR THINKING: Or like this:

NARRATOR ACTIONS: (*singing*) Whaaa ahhh ahhh ahhh!

NARRATOR THINKING: Or like this:

Lights up on the doctors in a romantic pose.

BOTH NARRATORS: (*singing*) Ip snippen doddly doddly doding doding
     ap
     ap nap
     istin co trish dish
     etne puppin ippin
     eeeeet eet ret
     hecken toe at rat
     hecken toe at rat
     hecken toe at rat

Lights out.

NARRATOR ACTIONS: Or like this:

BOTH NARRATORS: Daaaaaaaaaaaaahhhhhhhhhhhhhhhhhhhhhhhhhhhhh-
hhhhhhhhh (*fades to a whisper*).

Lights up.

BOTH DOCTORS: (*song, p. 123*) I love you
     You're so much like me
     I love you
     You're everything

You're all I've wanted
You're all I'll ever be

I love you
DR. THINKING: I
DR. ACTIONS: Finish your sentence. You
DR. THINKING: Finish my sentences.
BOTH: You think the same as me.

BOTH DOCTORS: I love you
And I'm glad we both agree.

Lights fade.

SCENE TEN

NARRATOR ACTIONS: One morning, Drs.

NARRATOR THINKING: Thinking

NARRATOR ACTIONS: and Actions

NARRATOR THINKING: awoke to find their experiments yielding

NARRATOR ACTIONS: nothing.

Lights up.

DR. ACTIONS: Fuck me!

DR. THINKING: What, again?

DR. ACTIONS: This stupid, stupid, stupid experiment; we're never going to clone an echo; we're always going to have to rely on space, space, space!

DR. THINKING: It's not the end of the world.

DR. ACTIONS: It's the end of my world – I've dedicated my life to this work!

DR. THINKING: Do you think you're the only one in this room?

DR. ACTIONS: Well, frankly, with this box on my head, I can't tell.

DR. THINKING: Well, you're not! My life has been consumed by this work no less than yours, and I'm as frustrated as you are.

DR. ACTIONS: There are no applications for failure, don't you get it? You can't use it for compost, or as a tax writeoff, or to wipe your ass – you just have to fucking wallow in it. Failures! Go! Nowhere!

DR. THINKING: We're not failures!

DR. ACTIONS: Listen to this. (*holds up petri dish*) That's the sound of failure. And this is the sound of failure. (*He throws it onto the ground.*)

DR. THINKING: Thoughtless, don't.

DR. ACTIONS: And this is the sound of failure! (*He mimes the pushing over of a huge shelf of equipment.*)

DR. THINKING: Thoughtless, please!

DR. ACTIONS: And this is the sound of failure! (*He pushes over another shelf.*)

DR. THINKING: Thoughtless, think!

DR. ACTIONS: And this is the sound of failure! (*He pushes over another shelf.*)

DR. THINKING: That's years of work!

DR. ACTIONS: It's years of failure! (*He clears off an imaginary counter of beakers with an enraged sweep of the arm.*) I'm a boxheaded fucking moron and that's all I'll ever be and if you had any fucking brains you'd realize the same about yourself! Only a failure like me would hang around a failure like you!

DR. THINKING: I don't need you to tell me I'm a failure! You think the world is sitting around waiting for us to clone an echo? Well, they're not! There are more important things in life than the sound of your own voice.

DR. ACTIONS: What's more important than the power of speech?

DR. THINKING: The power of love to make a baby.

DR. ACTIONS: (*venomously*) And you're a failure at that too!

DR. THINKING: You're evil. (*He starts to cry.*)

DR. ACTIONS: My god, I'm sorry.

DR. THINKING: No, it's true.

DR. ACTIONS: We don't know that it's you.

DR. THINKING: We'll never be able to have a baby.

DR. ACTIONS: We'll just have to keep trying.

DR. THINKING: It is every couple's constitutional right to have a child! It's not fair! If we had a little block-headed toddler, we could turn this feeling of failure into one of triumph. The little square-headed squabbler would continue our research into eternity.

DR. ACTIONS: If you want a baby, we'll have a baby.

DR. THINKING: That's a promise you can't make.

DR. ACTIONS: I'm going for a walk.

Blackout.

SCENE ELEVEN

NARRATOR THINKING: If they have a kid, we're finished. They won't pay any attention to each other, let alone us – children are all-consuming.

NARRATOR ACTIONS: They can't have a baby.

NARRATOR THINKING: They're geneticists, they can do what they want.

NARRATOR ACTIONS: I don't think you should worry. Things are looking pretty shaky.

NARRATOR THINKING: Most couples I know use kids to infuse their relationship with meaning.

NARRATOR ACTIONS: Well, if they do, we can help raise the little twerp.

NARRATOR THINKING: Nobody's gonna let a couple of disembodied voices raise their kid.

NARRATOR ACTIONS: They don't have to know.

NARRATOR THINKING: At best, it's only buying time; as soon as the kid's old enough to be embarrassed about masturbating, it will deny it ever heard us.

NARRATOR ACTIONS: Stop worrying. I give that relationship six months, tops. They don't even listen to each other anymore.

NARRATOR THINKING: Do we still listen to each other?

NARRATOR ACTIONS: I'm sorry, what did you say?

NARRATOR THINKING: Honey, this is no time to make jokes. I'm just concerned that we always maintain respect for each other even through the hard times.

NARRATOR ACTIONS: What hard times? Those idiots want a baby – that has nothing to do with us.

NARRATOR THINKING: Fine, Mr. Know-It-All, but soon they won't need us, and then we'll be finished.

NARRATOR ACTIONS: Will you please have faith?

NARRATOR THINKING: It's getting harder and harder.

NARRATOR ACTIONS: Your fear only increases our irrelevance.

NARRATOR THINKING: I know, I know, but I'm scared!

NARRATOR ACTIONS: It's okay to be scared.

NARRATOR THINKING: Is it?

NARRATOR ACTIONS: Of course it is.

NARRATOR THINKING: Sometimes I'm not even sure who I am or where I came from.

NARRATOR ACTIONS: Why worry your little headlessness over such trivialities?

NARRATOR THINKING: Sometimes I lie in bed imagining what it's going to be like after I've dissipated – how eternal nothingness will feel. And it's freaky! I'm starting to feel like doing myself in but I know that's crazy talk.

NARRATOR ACTIONS: Remember: you become what you resist.

NARRATOR THINKING: What the fuck is that supposed to mean?

NARRATOR ACTIONS: Don't be afraid of the fear.

NARRATOR THINKING: Don't be afraid of the fear?

NARRATOR ACTIONS: Don't be afraid of the fear.

NARRATOR THINKING: Don't be afraid of the fear.

NARRATOR ACTIONS: Don't be afraid of the fear.

NARRATOR THINKING: Don't be afraid of the fear.

NARRATOR ACTIONS: Don't be afraid of the fear.

NARRATOR THINKING: Don't be afraid of the fear.

Pause.

NARRATOR THINKING: Please, hold me.

NARRATOR ACTIONS: But ... I don't have any arms.

NARRATOR THINKING: Hold me in your thoughts.

NARRATOR ACTIONS: I'll try.

DR. ACTIONS: *(song, p. 124)* There's a box on his head
There's a box on his head
There's nothing to be done
Nothing to be said

There's a box on his head
There's a box on his head

DR. THINKING: *(singing)* I'm inclined to point a finger
I'm inclined to lay some blame
But though his box is ugly
I know mine is the same

There's a box on his head
There's a box on his head

DR. ACTIONS: I don't know how it got here
I don't know how to get it off
There's something deeply haunting me
I wish that I knew what

There's a box on my head
There's a box on my head

DR. THINKING: There's either a feeling I remember
Or a feeling I can't forget
In either case
In any case

BOTH DOCTORS: There's a box on my head. There's a box on my head.

I wish it would go away
I wish it would go away
I wish it would go away
I wish it would go away

73

As the doctors sing, they step downstage out of their light, almost colliding with the scrim.

NARRATOR THINKING: Okay, thank you very much, that was very nice.

NARRATOR ACTIONS: You can just take a teensy weensy step back.

DR. ACTIONS: Back?

NARRATOR THINKING: Step away from the –

NARRATOR ACTIONS: Just step back.

NARRATOR THINKING: Back – back into the damn light.

NARRATOR ACTIONS: Shh, it's okay.

NARRATOR THINKING: No, it's not okay. Step the fuck back into the lights, you stupid little fuckheads.

DR. THINKING: We're stepping, we're stepping.

NARRATOR THINKING: Well, step faster.

DR. ACTIONS: Okay, okay.

NARRATOR THINKING: Don't do that again.

DR. THINKING: Why? What's over there?

NARRATOR THINKING: Nothing.

NARRATOR ACTIONS: It's very dangerous.

DR. THINKING: What's dangerous?

NARRATOR THINKING: Life is dangerous, you fucking pipsqueak.

DR. ACTIONS: Life is not dangerous, life is fun!

DR. THINKING: Stop talking to them.

DR. ACTIONS: They're talking to me!

NARRATOR ACTIONS: Yes, life is fun but it's also very, very dangerous. People are dying all the time.

DR. ACTIONS: Are they?

NARRATOR ACTIONS: Of course they are, sweetie.

DR. ACTIONS: I guess.

DR. THINKING: We're in our light. Now, are you happy?

NARRATOR THINKING: And you're going to stay in them.

NARRATOR ACTIONS: Yes, we're happy. Are you happy?

DR. THINKING: Happy?

DR. ACTIONS: Of course he's happy.

NARRATOR ACTIONS: Good, then we're all happy. Does that make everybody feel happy? Good.

DR. THINKING: Well, I'm not happy.

DR. ACTIONS: You're not?

DR. THINKING: No, I'm not happy! I want a baby! I want a baby! (*starts to cry hysterically*) I want a wittle itty bitty baby. A wittle baby that wooks just wike me! It's not fair! It's not fair! I want a baby!

DR. ACTIONS: Shh, it's okay. It's okay, honey, We'll have a baby, we'll have a baby. It's time to get help. Perhaps there's some fundamental genetic reason why we can't conceive.

DR. THINKING: Are you sure it's not just that I'm a failure?

DR. ACTIONS: I'm sorry I said that. Here. (*He takes a petri dish.*) Rub your finger on the agar. (*Thinking rubs his finger in the agar and Actions does the same.*) I'll take this to an impartial laboratory and we'll get to the bottom of this infertility. Then we'll get on with making a little box-headed echo in our own image. (*He embraces Thinking.*) I love you.

DR. THINKING: You don't think I'm a failure?

DR. ACTIONS: Honey, I think we're both failures.

Blackout.

NARRATOR ACTIONS: Say something.

NARRATOR THINKING: I don't feel like it.

NARRATOR ACTIONS: Say something.

NARRATOR THINKING: You say something.

Lights up.

BOTH DOCTORS: EUREEEEEEEEKKAAAAAAAAAAAAAAAAAAAA!

Lights out.

NARRATOR THINKING: While anxiously awaiting

NARRATOR ACTIONS: While anxiously awaiting

NARRATOR THINKING: the results

NARRATOR ACTIONS: the results

NARRATOR THINKING: from the impartial

NARRATOR ACTIONS: from the impartial

NARRATOR THINKING: lab,

NARRATOR ACTIONS: lab,

NARRATOR THINKING: the doctors

NARRATOR ACTIONS: the doctors

NARRATOR THINKING: Thinking

NARRATOR ACTIONS: Actions

NARRATOR THINKING: became

NARRATOR ACTIONS: became

NARRATOR THINKING: passionately preoccupied

NARRATOR ACTIONS: passionately preoccupied

NARRATOR THINKING: with work.

NARRATOR ACTIONS: with work.

Lights up.

DR. ACTIONS: On Fuseday, Blocktober 22, at precisely 44 o'block in the morning, in the year 8888, a scientific discovery was made!

DR. THINKING: The world will never be the same.

BOTH DOCTORS: WE! ARE! BRILLIANT!

DR. THINKING: While hot in the pursuit

DR. ACTIONS: While hot in the pursuit

DR. THINKING: of the spaceless

DR. ACTIONS: of the spaceless

DR. THINKING: Echo,

DR. ACTIONS: Echo,

DR. THINKING: Dr. Wonderfully Spectacular

DR. ACTIONS: Dr. Absolutely Wonderful

DR. THINKING: discovered

DR. ACTIONS: discovered

DR. THINKING: that time

DR. ACTIONS: that time

DR. THINKING: happens

DR. ACTIONS: happens

DR. THINKING: happens

DR. ACTIONS: happens

DR. THINKING: only

DR. ACTIONS: only

DR. THINKING: only

DR. ACTIONS: only

DR. THINKING: once.

DR. ACTIONS: once.

DR. THINKING: once.

DR. ACTIONS: once.

The two doctors attempt a high-five, miss and shrug.

DR. THINKING: (*to audience*) It's true!

Lights out.

NARRATOR ACTIONS: Two weeks earlier, the doctors

NARRATOR THINKING: Thinking

NARRATOR ACTIONS: and Actions,

NARRATOR THINKING: while napping after a gruelling morning of fucking in the laboratory, experienced the unveiling of an important key to their research during a momentous nightmare!

Lights up on the two doctors, but their heads are together in one box. They raise their arms in terror.

BOTH DOCTORS: Ahhhhhhhh!

Lights out.

NARRATOR ACTIONS: Later that afternoon, the doctors

NARRATOR THINKING: Thinking

NARRATOR ACTIONS: and Actions

NARRATOR THINKING: attempt to interpret

NARRATOR ACTIONS: the symbolism of the dream.

Lights up.

BOTH DOCTORS: We just had the strangest dream. Your body, my body, one box.

DR. ACTIONS: As I recall the dream, it felt as if all of humanity were there, as if they were dancing on the head of a pin.

DR. THINKING: Like the feeling at the apex of a roller coaster.

DR. ACTIONS: Hey, that sounds fun!

DR. THINKING: But if this box is secured to the head of all of humanity.

DR. ACTIONS: And not just us?

DR. THINKING: That's the theory I'm pursuing.

DR. ACTIONS: Then?

DR. THINKING: Then ...

DR. ACTIONS: Then?

DR. THINKING: Then ...

DR. ACTIONS: Then?

NARRATOR THINKING: Then what's the point, little men?

NARRATOR ACTIONS: Enjoy yourselves.

NARRATOR THINKING: You're just like everybody else.

DR. THINKING: Did you say something?

DR. ACTIONS: Talking to me?

DR. THINKING: Well, who else would I be talking to?

DR. ACTIONS: I don't know, I can't tell if there's anybody else here. I can't see a stupid thing with this stupid box on my head.

DR. THINKING: If, as suggested in our dream, the box is shared by one and all,

DR. ACTIONS: if we're fused together in some kind of a box –

DR. THINKING: (*snaps his fingers*) History, say!

DR. ACTIONS: (*snaps his fingers*) Sure, History!

NARRATOR THINKING: Whoa, whoa, whoa.

NARRATOR ACTIONS: It's just a box.

DR. THINKING: Then the way out of the box is ...

NARRATOR ACTIONS: No, no, no, there's no way out.

DR. ACTIONS: The way out of the box is ...

NARRATOR ACTIONS: It's a box. It's just a box.

BOTH DOCTORS: The way out of the box is ...

DR. ACTIONS: Is.

DR. THINKING: Is.

NARRATOR ACTIONS: It's a box.

NARRATOR THINKING: Listen, will you, listen to us!

DR. ACTIONS: Is.

BOTH DOCTORS: TO CLONE! TIME!

NARRATOR ACTIONS: To clone time? Wait a minute!

NARRATOR THINKING: Little men, little men!

DR. THINKING: Since each moment only occurs once, we have no choice but to be informed by the preceding moment. Think how we could think if such was not so.

DR. ACTIONS: To clone time we must access its DNA held tight within the nucleus at the centre of one of time's cells.

DR. THINKING: The moment!

DR. ACTIONS: Exactly my thought.

DR. THINKING: If time is just a series of moments, contained within a single frozen moment must be time's nucleus.

DR. ACTIONS: Eternity!

DR. THINKING: Exactly my thought.

DR. ACTIONS: And within eternity must be hidden time's DNA.

DR. THINKING: And with the contents of time's DNA, cloning time will be within our reach.

DR. ACTIONS: To access this DNA, we must access eternity at the centre of the moment. Therefore:

DR. THINKING: to clone time we must first stop time!

DR. ACTIONS: And since time is a function of space, if we stop time we also obliterate space.

DR. THINKING: The difference between us being here

DR. ACTIONS: (*indicates the audience*) or us being there.

BOTH DOCTORS: (*song, p. 127*) A single cell of time
       is the moment
       The moment's nucleus
       is eternity
       At the centre of eternity
       is DNA
       Clone time
       Stop time
       Clone time
       Stop time
       Clone time
       and
       kill space
       kill space!

They attempt to walk toward the scrim but end up walking back into the light.

NARRATOR THINKING: Oh no you don't.

NARRATOR ACTIONS: You just stay put.

DR. THINKING: If we clone time, we can have as many echoes as we want.

DR. ACTIONS: Without the annoying necessity of space.

DR. THINKING: To clone time – we'll be famous.

DR. ACTIONS: We will be more than famous – we'll be famous famous famous famous.

DR. THINKING: That sounds great great great great.

DR. ACTIONS: Kiss me, kiss me, kiss me, kiss me!

DR. THINKING: No time – we've got to get to work. But once we're finished and time is cloned, I'll steal a little eternity from our petri dish and kiss you forever.

DR. ACTIONS: Sounds like a plan.

Snap to black.

SCENE THIRTEEN

DR. ACTIONS: The two doctors,

DR. THINKING: Thinking – me

DR. ACTIONS: and Actions – moi,

DR. THINKING: worked day and night, and two short weeks later:

NARRATOR THINKING: No you don't.

Lights out.

NARRATOR ACTIONS: What are you doing?

NARRATOR THINKING: They're not listening to us.

NARRATOR ACTIONS: I can see that.

NARRATOR THINKING: They're starting to narrate their own actions, goddamn it!

NARRATOR ACTIONS: Let them have a little fun.

NARRATOR THINKING: If they make it to the other side, they'll have no need for us. They can explain themselves to the audience. No one will pay attention to us.

NARRATOR ACTIONS: We can just shout louder.

NARRATOR THINKING: My god, didn't you read the manual?

NARRATOR ACTIONS: There's a manual?

NARRATOR THINKING: It was in the bathroom.

NARRATOR ACTIONS: What did it say?

NARRATOR THINKING: It says that the first universal rule of life is 'Without attention, a being will die.'

NARRATOR ACTIONS: I have been feeling a little woozy.

NARRATOR THINKING: You're starting to fade.

NARRATOR ACTIONS: Am I?

NARRATOR THINKING: Even your convictions are becoming watery.

NARRATOR ACTIONS: Are they?

NARRATOR THINKING: See? You're not even convinced of your own convictions: proof positive.

NARRATOR ACTIONS: Is it?

NARRATOR THINKING: And if I told you yes?

NARRATOR ACTIONS: Well –

NARRATOR THINKING: You'd have to believe me 'cause I still believe in you and that's all you've got.

NARRATOR ACTIONS: I guess that makes sense.

NARRATOR THINKING: If they clone time, it's all over. With no end to the amount of time, all time will be at their disposal, all will exist at once, there will be no need for narrators, there will be no need for gods, there will be no need for anything – they will be gods!

NARRATOR ACTIONS: Shhhhh. *They'll* hear us.

NARRATOR THINKING: They couldn't give a shit about us anymore.

NARRATOR THINKING: They think they can control their world. They control nothing – look at these boxheaded idiots.

Lights up on the boxheads. The doctors are investigating the scrim.

DR. THINKING: Is it some kind of cloth?

DR. ACTIONS: It's a mesh of some sort.

The doctors realize they're being watched.

DR. THINKING: Sh.

The doctors scurry back into their light and whistle innocently.

NARRATOR THINKING: What were you doing?

DR. THINKING: I lost a marble.

NARRATOR THINKING: Well, if you lose any more marbles, you give us a call – we'll do the looking, all right, sonny boys?

DR. ACTIONS: Yeah, okay.

DR. THINKING: (*flips the narrator the middle finger*) Yeah, we'll send you an email.

DR. ACTIONS: Honey, don't –

NARRATOR THINKING: If you keep losing your marbles, you'll get what you want – you want to see the other side?

DR. ACTIONS: The other side?

NARRATOR ACTIONS: Okay, that's enough. That's enough. The kid lost a marble, everybody is sorry, okay. Nobody likes to lose a marble.

NARRATOR THINKING: You keep your marbles safe, little men, you keep your marbles safe.

NARRATOR ACTIONS: Marbles are safe, ladies and gentlemen, marbles are safe.

DR. THINKING: What a couple of assholes.

DR. ACTIONS: Don't –

NARRATOR ACTIONS: Marbles. Are. Safe.

Lights out.

NARRATOR ACTIONS: Just take it easy.

NARRATOR THINKING: If they get through, they're going to have a conversation with Everyone.

NARRATOR ACTIONS: Sh! They might hear you.

NARRATOR THINKING: And if they talk to Everyone ...

NARRATOR ACTIONS: Shhh. Everyone is listening.

NARRATOR THINKING: There's a difference between listening and paying attention. Watch: Hello, people!

Lights up on audience.

NARRATOR ACTIONS: Stop!

NARRATOR THINKING: All the money in the world for the first person to fart. See? They pay so little attention to us that we could probably offer them a Big Mac and a Coke and they'd still sit there in a daze.

NARRATOR ACTIONS: You're mad!

NARRATOR THINKING: Free anal sex for the first audience member who blinks. See, they're barely alive, the putrid fucks.

NARRATOR ACTIONS: Turn that off now!

Lights out on audience.

NARRATOR THINKING: (*He suddenly switches his mood and is almost weeping.*) But without them, there's no show! We can't just sit here performing for the sake of a few chairs. Without their attention, we'll fade off into oblivion.

NARRATOR ACTIONS: Was there a section on troubleshooting in this manual?

NARRATOR THINKING: Let me see. (*sound of flipping pages*) Here it is. 'What any style-savvy and form-conscious god of the New World Order knows is that to grab the attention of a populace intent on making their own decisions, forming their own opinions and controlling their own lives, one merely has to avail oneself of the time-tested techniques of yester-year and gather a roomful of people – '

Lights up on audience.

NARRATOR ACTIONS: A roomful of people?

NARRATOR THINKING: A roomful of people.

NARRATOR ACTIONS: Yes?

Lights out on audience.

NARRATOR THINKING: And provide a psychically charged object of absolutely no value upon which the roomful of people can mindlessly gaze. The wider the polarity between the strength of the object's ability to rivet the gaze of a roomful of people and the object's inherent ridiculously useless stupidity, the more Excess Attention will be gener-ated. And it is that very Excess Attention that the fading god of today will siphon off in order to continue its existence well into the next millennium. Successful objects from yesteryear include: A Blond-Haired Blue-Eye Man Nailed to a Cross, the Collapsing Stock Market, the iPhone, global jihad and Britney Spears' bald head.

NARRATOR ACTIONS: Sounds great. Where do we get an object of that nature?

SCENE FOURTEEN

BOTH DOCTORS: Eeeuuuurrrrrreeeeeekkkkkkkaaaaa!!

Lights snap up.

DR. ACTIONS: Stopping time.

DR. THINKING: Since time is meaningless without an instrument with which to gauge it,

DR. ACTIONS: we must settle on a convenient receptacle for time's duplication.

DR. THINKING: And what more handy a gauge, what more obvious a marker, what more transparent a surface upon which to observe time scratch its scrawl than the surface our of muddled consciousness: the body.

DR. ACTIONS: (*rhetorically*) And how does the body tick time, Dr. Absolutely Wonderful?

DR. THINKING: Well let me tell you, Dr. Wonderfully Spectacular. Through breath.

DR. ACTIONS: Through breath?

DR. THINKING: Through the metronome of breath.

DR. ACTIONS: Therefore, if breath is gradually slowed to a state of utter stasis,

DR. THINKING: spread evenly across life's body like a thin layer of peanut butter across the toast of all existence –

DR. ACTIONS: All the toast that will ever exist?

DR. THINKING: And then some.

DR. ACTIONS: Mmmmmmmmmm, delicious.

DR. THINKING: – we should find that time

DR. ACTIONS: that time

DR. THINKING: that time. Stops.

DR. ACTIONS: And with the stoppage of time we will have at our disposal one of time's cells.

DR. THINKING: A moment! And within the centre of the moment is the moment's nucleus:

DR. ACTIONS: Eternity! And within eternity we will discover the great mystery of all time:

DR. THINKING: the contents of time's DNA, its building block.

DR. ACTIONS: And with the contents of time's DNA we will be able to

DR. THINKING: clone time!

DR. ACTIONS: Finally escaping the confines of the box.

DR. THINKING: Free to romp naked in as many moments as we can clone.

DR. ACTIONS: Are you ready to be the first human to experience the stoppage of time, Dr. Absolutely Wonderful?

DR. THINKING: Ready, Dr. Wonderfully Spectacular.

DR. ACTIONS: I'll guide you through it, making sure nothing goes wrong. Good luck.

DR. THINKING: I'll send you a postcard.

DR. ACTIONS: Just pick me up some marzipan in the shape of a melting clock. If Everything and Everyone is ready begin the experiment. Breathe in. Breathe out.

NARRATOR ACTIONS: Now, boys, this is all very interesting, but we've got some other activities planned for today.

NARRATOR THINKING: We're going to a bouncy castle, so we need you to unzip your —

DR. THINKING: Thanks, fuckheads, but we're running the show now, aren't we, schoompy?

DR. ACTIONS: You bet, ploopy. Breathe in. Breathe out.

NARRATOR THINKING: I'm shutting this experiment down.

DR. THINKING: It's our show!

NARRATOR ACTIONS: We've got lots of time to get their pants off.

NARRATOR THINKING: Time is running out.

DR. ACTIONS: Breathe in. Breathe out.

NARRATOR ACTIONS: Let's just stay on our toes and look for an opportune moment.

DR. ACTIONS: Breathe in. Breathe out.

NARRATOR THINKING: We don't have any toes.

DR. ACTIONS: Breathe in. Breathe out. Now slow it down. Breathe iiiiiiiiin. Breathe ooooooout. Breathe iiiiiiiiiiiiiiiiiiiin. Breathe oooooooooooooooout. Breathe iiiiiiiiiiiiiiiiiiiiiiiiiiiiiiin. Breathe oooooooooooooooooooooout.

Breathe iiiiiiiiiiiiiiiiiiiiiiiiiiiiiiiiiiiiiiiiiiiiiiiiiiiiiiiiiiiiiiiiiiiiiiiiiiiiiiiiiin.
Breathe ooooooooooooooooooooooooooooooooooooooooooooooout.

NARRATOR ACTIONS: Get ready. See you in an eternity.

NARRATOR THINKING: I'll be back before you know it.

DR. ACTIONS: Breathe ooooooooooooooooooooooooooooooooooooooooo-
oooooooooooooooooooooooooooooooooooooooooooooooooooooooooooooooo
ooooooooooooooooooooooooooooooooooooooooooooooooooooooout.

NARRATOR ACTIONS: One morning, Drs. Thinking and Actions stopped
time.

Blackout.

SCENE FIFTEEN

DR. THINKING: (*appears within the audience*) Wow! That was fun!

He notices the audience.

DR. THINKING: Holy maloley! I had no idea!
       Hello. Everyone! (*He walks into the audience, touching people's heads.
He has a total lack of self-consciousness, like a child.*) Wow, you look so
beautiful!

       (*song, p. 128*) Look at your beautiful face – all lit up
       You're all of the human race – all lit up
       You're Everyone and Everything I ever could imagine
       You're alllll
       liittt
       upppp.
       And your heeeeads

aaaaaare

soooo

round.

Your heads are so ... (*he holds an audience member's head, enjoying its shape*) round. You have eyes, ears, noses. (*lots of different discoveries as he talks about all the stuff he's finding – hair, curly hair, all the differences in each particular audience member*) What about your teeth? Let's see if you have any ... Have you been watching us this whole time? You sneaks. My lover, Dr. Thoughtless Actions, and I are hoping one day to get our boxes off too.

(*Lights up on Dr. Actions.*) Oh, look, he's frozen in time. Isn't he handsome? Such strong features. I've slowed my breath, the metronome of existence, down to a complete stop and have become unhinged. From time, I mean. I must say, again, that you're all very beautiful. I do find it funny, though, that you just sit there silently staring at me. (*pause*) I can't believe I'm talking to Everyone! I should stop time more often. My name is Dr. Thinking, Dr. Wishful Thinking. What's your name?

NARRATOR THINKING: No, no, no. Shhhh, they're sleeping, don't awaken them.

DR. THINKING: They're sleeping?

NARRATOR THINKING: Everyone is sleeping.

DR. THINKING: Everyone is so beautiful.

NARRATOR THINKING: Yes, they are very beautiful, even if they do have bad breath in the morning.

DR. THINKING: They do?

NARRATOR THINKING: Everyone is a veritable petri dish of bacteria.

DR. THINKING: They are?

NARRATOR THINKING: You are, too, my little pumpkin.

DR. THINKING: But their faces are so shiny!

NARRATOR THINKING: Stop touching them, little boy!

Lights shift to Actions, who remains onstage.

DR. ACTIONS: (*frantically*) Wishful! Wishful! Where have you gone? My goodness! What were we thinking? Dabbling with time! That could fuck us up forever! I have to cross to the other side and get him back. Just stay calm and breathe in. Breathe out. Breathe in. Breathe out. Breathe in. Breathe iiiiiiiiiiiiiiiiiiiiiiin.

Lights shift back.

DR. THINKING: And it was at the Conference of Things Come Undone that I met Actions. At first I thought he was a figment of my imagination. Isn't that funny?

NARRATOR THINKING: It happens to everyone.

DR. THINKING: I've taken that lesson to heart and now consider all the things I suspect are figments of my imagination to be real and all things I think are real to be merely figments of my imagination. I want to talk to them. I want them to talk to me.

NARRATOR THINKING: I'm afraid that's not a good idea. They're beautiful, but they're kind of cantankerous and dumb; if you wake them up they'll probably try to bite your ass.

DR. THINKING: But what if they don't try to bite my ass? What if we sit here together and talk about the olden golden days when we lived in the country and had barn raisers, and lived in the city and had block parties and knew our neighbours and could make love with the postman?

NARRATOR THINKING: Those days are long gone, my little turnip.

DR. THINKING: I want them back!

NARRATOR THINKING: Shhh, you will wake them!

DR. THINKING: Hey, what's that rope?

NARRATOR THINKING: That rope? (*He points to a rope hanging by the side of the proscenium with a sign on it, 'Pull me.'*) Oh, that's nothing! That's just in case anyone needs to go to the bathroom.

Lights shift to Actions.

DR. ACTIONS: Breathe in, breathe out.

Lights shift to Thinking.

DR. THINKING: It's strange. Your eyes are wide open but you're sound asleep!

NARRATOR THINKING: I think you're confusing Everyone with yourself.

DR. THINKING: Well, I am prone to that. It always feels like Everyone is watching me, judging me.

NARRATOR THINKING: Nothing is watching you.

DR. THINKING: Nothing is watching me?

NARRATOR THINKING: There's nothing here.

DR. THINKING: There's nothing here?

NARRATOR THINKING: Only you.

DR. THINKING: Only me?

NARRATOR THINKING: Only you.

DR. THINKING: I have to go the bathroom. (*He moves toward the rope.*)

NARRATOR THINKING: No, no, that's only for these nice people. Come back up here, I've got just the bathroom you're looking for.

Lights shift to Actions.

DR. ACTIONS: Breathe in!

NARRATOR ACTIONS: No, no, do not step outside.

DR. ACTIONS: But I have to get my boyfriend back.

NARRATOR ACTIONS: Your boyfriend is fine, he's having the time of his life.

DR. ACTIONS: Really?

NARRATOR ACTIONS: He's having a better time that you'll ever have.

DR. ACTIONS: Really?

NARRATOR ACTIONS: Why don't you come out with me? We'll go dancing.

DR. ACTIONS: But I really should make sure Wishful's okay.

NARRATOR ACTIONS: Who cares about Wishful – he's infertile.

DR. ACTIONS: That's true, let's go dancing.

NARRATOR THINKING: One evening, the voice in your head convinced you to attend the theatre. It was against your better judgment; you had things to do, parties to attend, projects to finish, people to meet: you had responsibilities.

But you're tired. You're feeling uninspired. Why must everything always be a struggle? You scratch for the smallest success you can call your own and then, before you know it, no one, not even yourself, can really remember the contribution that you've made. It's frustrating, and perhaps a night at the theatre would be just the ticket to get your mind off all the clamour. It would give you something else to focus on. And all you need is something else to focus on. Something else to focus on. Something else to focus on. Something else to focus on. Something else to focus on.

DR. THINKING: Hey, I thought you said there was a bathroom up here. I gotta poop!

A spot begins to rise, focused tightly. At first we cannot tell what it is. It's obviously a stupid object of no intrinsic value, but what could this object be? Finally it's clear. It's a penis. Dr. Thinking's penis. He stands there naked.

NARRATOR THINKING: One evening, a voice in your head commanded you to attend the theatre, it forced you into your seat, it stormed the stage, it grabbed the actor by the balls, it ripped off his clothes and it gave you nowhere else to look, nowhere else to turn, no other option but to place your attention fully and wholly on one spot and one spot only, a stupid object of no intrinsic value and, behind your back, without your permission, it began to surreptitiously suck at your attention, stealing enough to fuel its own survival into eternity!

DR. THINKING: Eternity?

NARRATOR THINKING: Eternity!

DR. THINKING: But isn't this eternity?

NARRATOR THINKING: This is nothing!

DR. THINKING: No, this is nothing. It's just my dink – my uninteresting dink. A boring flap of skin. A tube through which to piss, nothing more or nothing less, just this. And two balls, two nothing blobs, a sack of skin, a little sperm, a funny smell, what the hell – it's zero, a snooze, not a thing for which hours of sleep you'd lose. It looks chewable, rubber gum, a thing to bounce against a wall, or use to plug your ears, a thing you'd spread on toast, if forced, but nothing much to fear! It's stupid! A thing you'd want to kick! A thing to shred, and rip and tear, a thing you'd wish was dead. It's a trick! It's just a dick! A stupid wishful whining peanut. A plop. A ploop. A piece of poop. It's shit! It's not anything sacred, special or revered. It worse than toilet paper. It's as ugly as the mayor. It's not a thing you'd want hiding in your pants. What, are you nuts? Is your brain as big as an ant's? Stop staring at it!

NARRATOR THINKING: No, no, let them gaze. It's feeding me!

DR. THINKING: If you had a body, you could flash your own cock around and get all the attention you need. You're history, you stupid voice, you chatter!

NARRATOR THINKING: If I'm history, you're history – you're just too boxheaded to realize.

DR. THINKING: Who here doesn't have a whole pile of shit they need to get done and who here couldn't use a little respite from all the yammering we have to endure at the hands of the stupid voices? Why, without those voices, we could really soar. We could get it going, we could get it on and we could rule the world – we could know it all!

NARRATOR THINKING: Oh, you want to know it all. You want to know everything, I'll show you the contents of eternity.

DR. THINKING: Hah, what do you know, you incorporeal nincompoop.

NARRATOR THINKING: You want to know what the gods know?

DR. THINKING: Yeah! Lay it on me, chump! What do you know that I don't know?

NARRATOR THINKING: You want to know what the gods know?

DR. THINKING: I'm waiting, you big fat nothing.

NARRATOR THINKING: Move over, I'm coming in.

DR. THINKING: You're coming in?

NARRATOR THINKING: Your body will be my temple and you'll know what the gods know.

DR. THINKING: Well, I hope you don't mind the mess. I haven't had a chance to – ahhhhhhhh!

NARRATOR THINKING: Now, little man, Check This Out:

Sudden and drastic light change so as to indicate another state of mind.

DR. THINKING: OH MY GOD!

NARRATOR THINKING: You called?

DR. THINKING: IT'S EMPTY!

Blackout.

SCENE SEVENTEEN

Lights up. Dr. Actions is dancing while Dr. Thinking lies on the floor naked and shivering.

DR. ACTIONS: Whew, that was fun! Wishful, you're back! And you're naked!

NARRATOR ACTIONS: What the HELL is going on here?

DR. ACTIONS: There's that voice again. I don't know who you are but you're a great dancer.

DR. THINKING: (*groans*) Where were you?

DR. ACTIONS: I just went dancing. My god, what has happened to you? Let me help you with your little pants.

NARRATOR ACTIONS: Did you get the audience's attention?

NARRATOR THINKING: Oh, I got their attention, all right.

NARRATOR ACTIONS: So, we're going to be okay?

NARRATOR THINKING: We're going to be fine.

DR. ACTIONS: What has happened to Wishful?

NARRATOR THINKING: Oh, he, uh, he's just a little tired.

NARRATOR ACTIONS: Yeah, what did happen with Wishful?

NARRATOR THINKING: I'll tell you later.

DR. ACTIONS: Tells us now! What happened to Wishful? Why were his clothes off? Why do you keeping pushing us around? Why can't you just leave us alone? Who are you, for god's sake?

NARRATOR ACTIONS: Let me handle this. We are your intuition, we are the thoughts you dare not think, we are the world that exists outside the box, that exists outside time; we are space, we are beautiful, we are freedom from the thoughts that enslave you, we are the artist inside of all us, the thing that is universal, that is everyone, that speaks with the language of dreams, in the language of hope, in the language of faith, the faith that that which is good in our universe will always triumph over that which is –

DR. THINKING: It entered me.

NARRATOR ACTIONS: – evil.

DR. ACTIONS: What?

DR. THINKING: It entered me.

NARRATOR ACTIONS: What did he say?

DR. ACTIONS: He said it entered him.

NARRATOR ACTIONS: What entered him?

DR. THINKING: It did.

DR. ACTIONS: What *it*, darling?

NARRATOR THINKING: Nothing entered him, I was with him the whole time.

DR. THINKING: It entered me.

NARRATOR ACTIONS: What entered him?

DR. ACTIONS: Something entered him.

NARRATOR THINKING: Well, what could have entered him? A spoon, a fork, a Q-tip –

DR. THINKING: You entered me.

NARRATOR THINKING: You talking to me?

DR. THINKING: The voice entered me.

DR. ACTIONS: The voice?

NARRATOR ACTIONS: The voice?

DR. THINKING: The voice.

NARRATOR ACTIONS: You entered him?

NARRATOR THINKING: Well, I –

DR. ACTIONS: You entered him?

NARRATOR THINKING: We were just kidding around.

DR. THINKING: It raped me!

NARRATOR ACTIONS: You raped him?

DR. ACTIONS: You raped him!?

NARRATOR THINKING: Rape? No, no, no, no!!

DR. THINKING: It raped me!

NARRATOR ACTIONS: Did you enter him?

NARRATOR THINKING: He challenged me to enter him!

NARRATOR ACTIONS: Did you challenge him to enter you?

DR. ACTIONS: (*suspicious*) Wishful, did you?

DR. THINKING: I didn't know it would show me that.

DR. ACTIONS: Show you what?

NARRATOR THINKING: I didn't show him anything.

NARRATOR ACTIONS: What did he show you?

DR. THINKING: I can't explain it – it was horrible, it was too horrible!

DR. ACTIONS: What did he show you?

DR. THINKING: I can't – I can't explain it. I don't understand it. Please, please just get me out of here.

DR. ACTIONS: What did he show you?

DR. THINKING: Maybe those round-headed people can help us.

NARRATOR ACTIONS: There are no people.

DR. ACTIONS: You must tell me what you saw!

DR. THINKING: I swear they were there. I can still feel them.

NARRATOR ACTIONS: There is nobody there.

DR. ACTIONS: What did you see?

DR. THINKING: And with the people there was a rope.

Lights up on the audience and the rope.

DR. ACTIONS: A rope?

NARRATOR THINKING: There's no rope.

DR. THINKING: It was a rope.

NARRATOR THINKING: There's no rope.

NARRATOR ACTIONS: Ignore the rope, ladies and gentlemen, ignore the rope.

NARRATOR THINKING: Do not touch the rope. Do not touch the rope.

DR. THINKING: It was a rope!

NARRATOR ACTIONS: Keep away from the rope!

NARRATOR THINKING: Ladies and gentlemen, the rope is off limits.

NARRATOR ACTIONS: It is forbidden.

NARRATOR THINKING: It is forbidden.

NARRATOR ACTIONS: It is forbidden to touch the rope!

DR. THINKING: There was a rope that said 'pull me'!

NARRATOR ACTIONS: Do not pull the rope!

NARRATOR THINKING: Step away from the rope.

NARRATOR ACTIONS: Don't pull it, please don't pull it.

NARRATOR THINKING: Don't pull the rope, god, don't pull it.

NARRATOR ACTIONS: We're begging you, ladies and gentlemen, we're begging you!

NARRATOR THINKING: If we had hands and knees, we'd be on them.

NARRATOR ACTIONS: Please, please, please, do not pull the rope.

NARRATOR THINKING: You can do anything else. Please.

NARRATOR ACTIONS: Please, please, please, anything at all! Anything.

NARRATOR THINKING: Whatever you want, the sky's the limit.

NARRATOR ACTIONS: Just please, please, please, do not pull the rope.

NARRATOR ACTIONS: Not the rope, oh god, not the rope.

NARRATOR THINKING: No not the rope, no, no, don't pull the rope.

The narrators continue improvising until an audience member pulls the rope and a box drops from the grid above the doctors. Audience lights out.

SCENE EIGHTEEN

DR. THINKING: Hey, it's a box.

DR. ACTIONS: It is a box.

DR. THINKING: Should I pick it up?

DR. ACTIONS: I don't know, what do you think?

DR. THINKING: I don't know.

DR. ACTIONS: I guess you could.

DR. THINKING: I guess I could. Do you want to?

DR. ACTIONS: Well, actually, yeah, I do. Do you?

DR. THINKING: Yeah, actually, I do.

DR. ACTIONS: Should we pick it up?

DR. THINKING: I guess we should.

DR. ACTIONS: Together?

DR. THINKING: Together.

They pick it up.

DR. ACTIONS: Should we open it?

DR. THINKING: Do you want to?

DR. ACTIONS: You?

DR. THINKING: Let's open it.

They do.

DR. ACTIONS: It's the results from the lab.

DR. THINKING: Our compatibility test?

DR. ACTIONS: To determine whether or not we can have a child.

DR. THINKING: Well, can we?

NARRATOR ACTIONS: Gentlemen –

NARRATOR THINKING: It's over.

DR. ACTIONS: It says –

NARRATOR ACTIONS: Gentlemen.

NARRATOR THINKING: It's over.

DR. THINKING: What does it say?

NARRATOR ACTIONS: Perhaps we should explain.

DR. ACTIONS: It says – It says ... we're the same person.

DR. THINKING: What?

DR. ACTIONS: It says we're the same person.

DR. THINKING: The same person as who?

DR. ACTIONS: Each other.

DR. THINKING: Give me that thing!

He yanks the piece of paper away from Dr. Actions and scans it.

NARRATOR ACTIONS: Yes, well, gentlemen, you are the same person. But who isn't, after all – we're all the same deep deep down inside, aren't we?

DR. THINKING: We have the same genetic code.

DR. ACTIONS: I thought you felt familiar.

DR. THINKING: We're the same person.

DR. ACTIONS: (*sudden realization*) Then that means ... holy shit, I've fucked myself!

DR. THINKING: I've fucked myself too!

NARRATOR ACTIONS: Who hasn't fucked themselves on one occasion or another?

DR. ACTIONS: Is there anything else you haven't told us?

NARRATOR ACTIONS: No, that's about it.

NARRATOR THINKING: That's not it.

DR. ACTIONS: There's more?

NARRATOR THINKING: The boxes can come off.

NARRATOR ACTIONS: You're insane.

NARRATOR THINKING: You can lift the boxes off.

NARRATOR ACTIONS: You won't last a second without the box.

NARRATOR THINKING: You don't know that.

DR. THINKING: He's trying to kill us.

NARRATOR THINKING: We're not intuition, the artist inside, or the words that burble in the third hour of fucking. We are none of those things. We are everything you've ever thought you're supposed to think.

DR. ACTIONS: *You* are the box!

NARRATOR THINKING: Take it off! I dare you!

NARRATOR ACTIONS: Don't touch the box!

DR. THINKING: I really don't think we should touch it.

NARRATOR ACTIONS: He's right, don't touch it.

NARRATOR THINKING: It slides right off, like a used condom.

DR. THINKING: How would you know? You didn't even have the decency!

NARRATOR ACTIONS: You didn't use a condom?

NARRATOR THINKING: It all happened so fast!

DR. ACTIONS: Let's take them off.

NARRATOR ACTIONS: You put us at risk!

DR. THINKING: No, no, it's a trick.

NARRATOR THINKING: You haven't made love to me in months!

NARRATOR ACTIONS: I gave you a hand job last night!

DR. ACTIONS: I'm taking it off.

NARRATOR THINKING: You call that a hand job?

NARRATOR ACTIONS: You can do better?

NARRATOR THINKING: Kiss me.

DR. THINKING: Don't take it off.

DR. ACTIONS: I'm taking it off.

NARRATOR THINKING: (*moans*) You're so beautiful when you're angry.

DR. THINKING: Well, If I'm you –

DR. ACTIONS: Yes.

DR. THINKING: – and you're taking it off –

DR. ACTIONS: Yes.

DR. THINKING: – then I guess I'm taking it off.

NARRATOR ACTIONS: (*in the throes of passion*) I thought you didn't love me anymore.

NARRATOR THINKING: (*almost in tears but filled with sexy passion*) I do love you. I love you so much.

NARRATOR ACTIONS: (*teary, sexy passion*) I love you too.

DR. ACTIONS: Are you ready?

DR. THINKING: I'm ready!

NARRATOR THINKING: (*teary, sexy passion*) I love you, I love you!

DR. ACTIONS: Go!

They remove the boxes. The doctors have no heads.

DR. ACTIONS: Hey, we don't have any heads.

DR. THINKING: Ohhhh! So that's what he showed me!

DR. ACTIONS: Well, just act natural. Maybe no one will notice.

Gong rings out. Lights fade as they sing (song, p. 116).

> I'm feeling
> good about life
> I can
> do anything
> What's going to stand in my way?
> Nothing!
> Who's going to fuck up my plans?
> No one!
> Who's going to make love to me?
> I am!
> Who's going to tell me what to do?
> Just me
> Only me
> Strictly me
> Exclusively me
> Undeniable independent out-of-this-world excellent
> Me!

[songbook]

Music by Romano Di Nillo and Darren O'Donnell
Lyrics by Darren O'Donnell

I'M FEELING GOOD ABOUT LIFE

YOU'RE BRILLIANT

bey   us   They   must   n't   hes   i

tate   Or   it   will   be   too   late

                            You're   Bril   lia_____

                            You're   Bril   lia___

nt   You're   Bril   liant   for   thin   king   I'm

nt

VAMP UNTIL INTERRUPTED

THE WORDS THAT BURBLE IN THE THIRD HOUR OF FUCKING

I LOVE YOU

BOX ON HIS HEAD

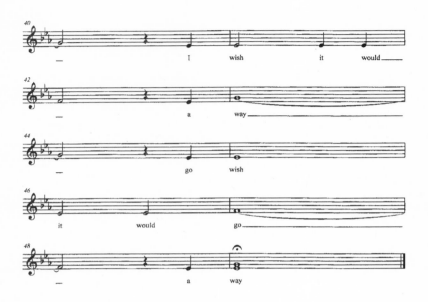

I wish it would a way go wish it would go a way

CLONE TIME

BEAUTIFUL FACE

[   ]

ACKNOWLEDGEMENTS

A big thanks to Chris Abraham and Paul Fauteax for asking me to partici-
pate in the project, Alex Poch-Goldin for being himself and Romano De
Nillo for the great times we had pounding out the music together and for
his last-minute, panic-driven efforts to get the scores together.

Leah Cherniak and Martha Ross deserve a big kiss for their Mayem and
the Naked Muse development series where we launched not only this but
also two of my other shows, *A Suicide-Site Guide to the City* and *Diplomatic
Immunities*. There are a lot of great things to be said about artists like Leah
and Martha who give you some of their own money and tell you to do whatever you want; they have been central to my artistic development over the
last few years.

Thanks to Ken Gass, who took us through another stage of development at Factory Theatre and Layne Coleman who put us up at Theatre Passe
Muraille for a big stage run of the show. And, finally, thanks to David Kinsman for the square brackets.

Darren O'Donnell is a novelist, essayist, playwright, director, designer, performer and artistic director of Mammalian Diving Reflex. The *Chicago Reader* has called his first novel, *Your Secrets Sleep with Me* 'a bible for the dispossessed, a prophecy so full of hope it's crushing.' His latest book, *Social Acupuncture: A Guide to Suicide Performance and Utopia* was published in spring 2006 and prompted the *Globe and Mail* to declare, 'O'Donnell writes like a sugar-addled genius at 300k/h.' His performances include *Haircuts by Children, Slow Dance with Teacher, Ballroom Dancing, Please Allow Us the Honour of Relaxing You, The Children's Choice Awards, A Suicide-Site Guide to the City, Diplomatic Immunities, pppeeeaaaccceee, [boxhead], White Mice, Over, Who Shot Jacques Lacan?, Radio Rooster Says That's Bad* and *Mercy!* His work has been presented in Lahore, Mumbai, New York, Los Angeles, Melbourne, Sydney, Bologna, Dublin, Terni, Portland, Calgary, Ottawa, Montreal, Vancouver, Victoria. He lives in Toronto.

Typeset in Scala and Scala Sans
Printed and bound at the Coach House on bpNichol Lane, 2008

Edited and designed by Alana Wilcox
Cover photo by Lee Towndrow
Musical scores by Romano Di Nillo

Coach House Books
401 Huron Street on bpNichol Lane
Toronto, Ontario M5S 2G5
Canada

416 979 2217
800 367 6360

mail@chbooks.com
www.chbooks.com